# BREAD MAKING COOKBOOK

The Complete Guide to Success in Preparing Keto Bread With Weight Loss

(Easy Keto Bread Recipes for Weight Loss)

**Kevin Humble**

Published by Alex Howard

© **Kevin Humble**

All Rights Reserved

*Bread Making Cookbook: The Complete Guide to Success in Preparing Keto Bread With Weight Loss (Easy Keto Bread Recipes for Weight Loss)*

**ISBN 978-1-990169-31-1**

All rights reserved. No part of this guide may be reproduced in any form without permission in writing from the publisher except in the case of brief quotations embodied in critical articles or reviews.

**Legal & Disclaimer**

The information contained in this book is not designed to replace or take the place of any form of medicine or professional medical advice. The information in this book has been provided for educational and entertainment purposes only.

The information contained in this book has been compiled from sources deemed reliable, and it is accurate to the best of the Author's knowledge; however, the Author cannot guarantee its accuracy and validity and cannot be held liable for any errors or omissions. Changes are periodically made to this book. You must consult your doctor or get professional medical advice before using any of the suggested remedies, techniques, or information in this book.

# Table of contents

**PART 1** .................................................................................................. 1

**INTRODUCTION** ................................................................................. 2

- Onion Bread With Cheese .................................................................. 3
- Poppy Cake .......................................................................................... 5
- Bread In A Frying Pan ........................................................................ 7
- Quick Bread In The Frying Pan ........................................................ 8
- Bread On Semolina ............................................................................ 9
- Unleavened Bread From Rye Flour ............................................... 10
- Bread On Serum Without Yeast .................................................... 11
- Banana Bread With Walnuts ......................................................... 12
- Bread At Leaven ............................................................................... 13
- Bread From Green Buckwheat ...................................................... 14
- Armenian Bread ............................................................................... 15
- Sour Bread ........................................................................................ 16
- Brewed Bread ................................................................................... 17
- Banana Bread ................................................................................... 18
- Bread In A Slow Cooker ................................................................. 19
- Filling Bread ..................................................................................... 21
- Unheated Bread In A Slow Cooker ............................................... 22
- Bread Without Yeast ....................................................................... 23
- French Bread .................................................................................... 24
- Bread In A Slow Cooker ................................................................. 25
- Bread "Pita" ...................................................................................... 26
- Gray Bread ........................................................................................ 27
- Bread In The Oven .......................................................................... 29
- Whole-Grain Bread In The Oven ................................................... 30
- Whole-Wheat Bread On Kefir ....................................................... 31
- Bread On Mashed Potatoes ........................................................... 32
- Wheat-Rye Bread In The Oven ...................................................... 33
- Round Bread .................................................................................... 34
- Grain Bread ...................................................................................... 35
- Bread By Dyukan ............................................................................. 36

| | |
|---|---|
| Bread On Kefir On Yeast | 37 |
| Bread On Kefir In A Bread Maker | 38 |
| Wheat Bread With Rye Starter | 39 |
| Onion Bread In The Oven | 40 |
| Quick Bread In The Oven | 41 |
| Bread With Dry Yeast In A Slow Cooker | 42 |
| Amaranth Bread | 43 |
| Wheat-Rye Bread In The Bread Maker | 44 |
| Homemade Wheat Bread In The Oven | 45 |
| Whole-Grain Bread Without Yeast In The Oven | 46 |
| Bread "Taba-Nan" | 47 |
| English Muffin Rolls | 48 |
| Norwegian Grain Breads | 49 |
| Roll With Poppy Seeds | 50 |
| Buns With Garlic | 51 |
| Whole-Wheat Loaves With Bran On Kefir | 53 |
| Chocolate Bun | 54 |
| The Custard Cake | 55 |
| Cottage Cheese Cake Without Yeast | 57 |
| Homemade Bread | 58 |
| Bread With Spinach | 59 |
| Bread With Bran In A Bread Maker | 60 |
| Thin Focaccia On Ricotta | 61 |
| Whole-Grain Bread With Acetane | 62 |
| Focaccia With Fried Onions And Cheese | 63 |
| White Bread On Sunflower Oil | 64 |
| Australian Unleavened Bread | 65 |
| Toast Bread | 66 |
| Bread From Baking Mixture | 67 |
| Classic Homemade Borodino Bread In The Oven | 68 |
| Focaccia With Cherry And Provencal Herbs | 69 |
| Bread On Kefir With Mustard And Mayonnaise | 70 |
| Bread On Kefir Without Yeast | 71 |
| Italian Bread | 72 |
| Whole-Grain Buns | 73 |
| Apple Bread On Mayonnaise | 74 |

| | |
|---|---|
| OATMEAL BREAD IN THE BREAD MAKER | 75 |
| HOMEMADE LOAF ON KEFIR | 76 |
| VIENNESE BAGUETTES | 77 |
| BATON IS PORTIONED | 78 |
| DOUGH FOR TARTLETS | 79 |
| WHEAT HOME NOODLES | 80 |
| CAKE WITH SOUR CREAM WITH CANDIED FRUIT | 81 |
| FAST CAKE IN THE BREAD MAKER | 82 |
| EASTER COTTAGE CHEESE CAKE | 83 |
| ROMAN FOCACCIA | 84 |
| WHEAT BREAD IN A BREADMAKER | 85 |
| BURRITO WITH RICE | 86 |
| WHEAT STARTER FOR BREAD | 87 |
| UNLEAVENED BREAD IN THE OVEN | 88 |
| MUSTARD BREAD | 89 |
| LEAVEN FOR UNLEAVENED BREAD | 90 |
| DOUGH FOR HOMEMADE NOODLES | 91 |
| WHITE BREAD IN THE OVEN | 92 |
| BREAD WITH RYE BRAN | 93 |
| BREAD WITH MATCHA TEA | 94 |
| DOUGH DUMPLINGS IN A BREADMAKER | 95 |
| BREAD LINZ | 96 |
| EGG NOODLES | 97 |
| BREAD IN GREEK YOGHURT | 98 |
| UKRAINIAN DUMPLINGS | 99 |
| WHEAT-RYE BREAD WITH NUTS | 100 |
| ARMENIAN LAVASH | 101 |
| BUNS "ROSES" | 102 |
| BREAD FORMING | 103 |
| BREAD "MATNAKASH" | 104 |
| CLARET "TEMPURA" | 105 |
| WHITE BREAD IN A BREAD MAKER | 106 |
| BREAD FROM WHEAT FLOUR WITH HONEY | 107 |
| BAGUETTES WITH WHOLE WHEAT FLOUR AND BRAN | 108 |
| **PART 2** | **109** |

| | |
|---|---|
| INTRODUCTION | 110 |
| **CHAPTER 1: KETOGENIC BREAD RECIPES** | **111** |
| LOW CARB KETO "CORNBREAD" | 111 |
| CHEESE AND JALAPEÑO BREAD | 112 |
| KETO BREAD | 114 |
| LOW CARB BAGELS | 115 |
| MEAT BAGEL | 117 |
| LOW CARB PIZZA CRUST | 118 |
| LOW CARB PIZZA | 119 |
| 2-MINUTE LOW CARB ENGLISH MUFFINS | 121 |
| FLOURLESS EGG AND COTTAGE CHEESE SAVORY BREAKFAST MUFFINS | 123 |
| MORNING MEATLOAF | 125 |
| LOW CARB MEAT LOAF | 127 |
| KETO BREADSTICKS | 129 |
| CHEESY CAULIFLOWER BREADSTICKS | 131 |
| OOPSIES | 133 |
| AIP BREAD ROLLS | 134 |
| DINNER ROLL | 135 |
| KETO BUNS | 136 |
| STRAWBERRY SHORTCAKE | 138 |
| BLUEBERRY LEMON MUFFINS | 140 |
| CHOCOLATE COVERED MACAROONS | 142 |
| PESTO KETO CRACKERS | 144 |
| CHEESY PARTY CRACKERS | 146 |
| MICROWAVE BREAD (1) | 148 |
| CINNAMON SWIRL BREAD | 149 |
| KETO BREAD LOAVES BREAD | 151 |
| FOCACCIA STYLE FLAX BREAD | 152 |
| COCONUT TORTILLAS | 153 |
| ALMOND FLOUR TORTILLAS | 154 |
| CHEESY GARLIC BREAD | 155 |
| ZUCCHINI BREAD | 157 |
| LOW CARB SOFT PRETZELS | 159 |
| LOW CARB BAGEL DOGS OR PRETZEL DOGS | 161 |
| MINI PANCAKE DONUTS | 163 |

| | |
|---|---|
| Chocolate Donuts | 164 |
| Chocolate Waffles | 166 |
| Bread Crumbs | 167 |
| Garlic Bread | 168 |
| Flourless Chocolate Cake | 170 |
| Low Carb Flat Bread | 172 |
| Coconut Flour Flatbread | 174 |
| Microwave Bread (2) | 175 |
| Breakfast Biscuit | 176 |
| Crackers | 177 |
| Herb Bread | 178 |
| Fluffy Keto Pancake / Waffle | 179 |
| Carrot Cake Loaf | 181 |
| Rosemary Coconut Savory Bread | 183 |
| Thanksgiving Bread | 184 |
| Bulletproof Bread | 186 |
| **CONCLUSION** | **187** |

# Part 1

# Introduction

Bread is a product that is produced by baking, steaming or frying dough; it consists of (minimum) water and flour. This product is an important part of a balanced diet; it provides the body with energy and promotes growth and development. The product contains a huge amount of useful substances: B vitamins, selenium, niacin, iron, phosphorus, magnesium, calcium, copper, dietary fiber. Bread is often served in the first and second courses; it is perfectly combined with meat, vegetables, and soups. Can use it as an independent dish. In this book you will find a detailed description of a variety of bread recipes that are easy to prepare at home.

# Onion Bread With Cheese

**Ingredients:**
- Rural milk - 1 glass
- Yeast, fresh - 10 g
- Wheat Flour - 6 table loques
- Sugar - 1 tablespoon
- Wheat flour - 300 g + dust
- Salt - 1 teaspoonful
- Egg of chicken - 1 piece
- Sunflower oil - 50 ml
- Onion - 1 head
- Cheese hard - 50-75 g
- Sunflower oil - for frying

**Preparation:**
1. In a bowl, crumbled fresh pressed yeast. Let's dissolve fresh yeast in warm country milk. Thoroughly mix the milk with the yeast. Add the wheat flour to the quick crust. We mix it with a whisk. Let's add sugar. Again we mix well. Let's leave the incense in the heat for fermentation for 30-45 minutes.
2. As bubbles appear, add 300 g of flour to our blisters. We split the warm chicken egg. We pour sunflower oil. Do not forget to salt. Stir the dough until smooth.
3. We cover the container with the test package or food film. We lubricate the inner side of the package with sunflower oil. We leave in the heat to increase in volume 3-4 times.
4. We lower the dough down. Add the fried onions. Next is grated cheese. The dough should be gently mixed.
5. Form the dough into a bun, and then slightly flatten it. Put the bun on the paper for baking, and then on the baking tray. Grease the paper with sunflower oil.
6. We bake homemade onion bread with cheese in a oven heated up to 240 ° C for at least 60 minutes. And the first 20

minutes the heating temperature should be maximum, and then reduced to 180-200 ° C.

7. To the hat did not burn, cover the bread with a sheet of foil. We remove the finished bread on a metal mesh. We cover with a towel. Let's cool down.

# Poppy Cake

**Ingredients:**
- Sugar - 50 g
- Wheat flour - 80 g
- Dry yeast - 7 g
- Milk is warm - 160 ml
- The whole
- Yolks of chicken eggs - 4 pieces
- Sugar - 70 g
- Salt
- Wheat flour - 350-370 g
- The water is warm - 75 ml
- Butter - 80 g
- Poppy - 100 g
- Sugar - 75 g
- Proteins of chicken eggs - 1 piece

**Preparation:**
1. Preparing the sponge. Mix flour, sugar, yeast, add warm milk, cover with a film and leave in a warm place for 20-30 minutes. Add yolks, salt, sugar and flour to it. We knead the dough. Cover the film and leave in a warm place for 30 minutes.
2. After half an hour, add warm water. We knead the dough to homogeneity. Then we introduce a softened butter. And again we knead it to smoothness. Cover with a film and leave in a warm place for 1-2 hours.
3. We spread it on the working surface, hands and surface lubricate with sunflower oil. The dough is stretched into a rectangle, then folded three times along and three times across. So do two more times. We put it in the bowl, cover it with a film and again in a warm place for 1-1,5 hours.
4. Dough lay on the work surface, hands lubricate with oil. Divide the dough into the number of forms you have. Lubricate the

filling. For her, you just need to grind the poppy in a coffee grinder, add the powdered sugar and protein. Mix.

5. Then roll the roll from the smaller side, bend the rolls in half and put them in folds upwards.

6. Cover the forms with a film and send it to a warm place for 30-60 minutes. We send the form to the oven heated to 200 degrees for 30 minutes.

# Bread In A Frying Pan

**Ingredients:**
- Whey Milk - 200 ml
- Salt - 1 teaspoon
- Sugar - 1 teaspoon
- Soda - 1 teaspoon
- Egg - 1 piece
- Flour - 400 g
- Vegetable oil - for frying

**Preparation:**
1. Sift flour into a bowl of suitable size. Add salt, sugar and soda. Mix well.
2. In the dry ingredients, drive in the egg and pour the milk serum at room temperature. Stir with a spoon, and then knead the dough with your hands.
3. Lubricate the bowl with vegetable oil, lay out the dough, cover with a towel and leave "rest" for 30 minutes.
4. Using a silicone brush, lubricate the frying pan with a thin layer of vegetable oil.
5. Put the prepared dough on a cold frying pan, hands spread it on the bottom. Should be a cake with a thickness of about 2 cm. Send the pan with bread to the fire, cover tightly with a lid and fry over a very slow fire for 25 minutes.
6. Then gently turn over and fry another 25 minutes on the other side, under the lid.

# Quick Bread In The Frying Pan

**Ingredients:**
- Kefir 250 g
- Egg - 2 pieces
- Soft cheese - 200 g
- Flour - 7 tablespoons
- Salt - 2 g
- Sugar - 1 tablespoon
- Mustard oil - 3 tablespoons
- Soda - 1 teaspoon

**Preparation:**
1. In a deep bowl, combine the eggs, salt and sugar. Beat.
2. Pour in kefir. And immediately pour mustard oil. Thoroughly mix everything.
3. Mild cheese into a small crumb and put into a bowl. Slightly mix and immediately pour in soda.
4. Gently mix the mass and pour the sifted flour. Gently stirring, bring the mass to homogeneity.
5. Preheat the frying pan, pour a spoonful of mustard oil and immediately pour the dough there. Cover with a lid and cook for 15-20 minutes at the lowest heat.
6. Then turn very gently to the other side and continue cooking the fast bread in the frying pan as much as it does.

# Bread On Semolina

**Ingredients:**
- Wheat flour - 90 g
- Yeast, fresh - 2 g
- Wheat flour - 90 g
- Semolina - 120 g
- Vegetable oil - 1,5 tablespoons
- Salt - 1 teaspoon
- Yeast, fresh - 5 g

**Preparation:**
1. Opara. Yeast diluted in water, add flour, mix. Cover with a towel.
2. For yeast, dilute in water. Leave to stand for 10 minutes. Add semolina, oil and salt. Mix. Add the spoon.
3. Pour out the flour, mix until homogeneous. Leave for 10 minutes.
4. On the table, pour a little flour, knead the dough for 10 minutes. Cover and leave for lifting.
5. After form a bun. Put a baking tray with flour, put our bollocks, sprinkle with flour. Cover with a napkin and leave for 30 minutes in the warmth.
6. Bake bread "Kolobok" at a temperature of 180 degrees 30-40 minutes, until ruddy.

# Unleavened Bread From Rye Flour

**Ingredients:**
- Flour rye - 400 g
- Milk whey - 1.5 cups
- Salt - 1 teaspoon
- Sugar - 1 tablespoon
- Vegetable oil - 2 tablespoons
- Flax seeds - 3 tablespoons
- Baking Powder - 11 g

**Preparation:**
1. In a deep bowl, sift flour with baking powder, add sugar and salt.
2. Serum slightly warmed, add to the flour, pour linseed, and pour oil.
3. Knead soft dough, not glued to the hands. If necessary, we grease hands with vegetable oil. Cover the dough with a food film and let it stand in a warm place for 30-40 minutes.
4. The mold for baking is sprinkled with flour, we spread the formed bread, it is also sprinkled lightly with flour, and we make cuts from above. Preheat the oven to 200 degrees, put the form on the bottom of the oven with water, and send the bread for 15 minutes. After a while, we reduce the temperature to 180 degrees and bake rye bread for another 40-50 minutes.

# Bread On Serum Without Yeast

**Ingredients:**
- Wheat-rye flour - 2 cups
- Whey Milk - 1 cup
- Salt - 0.5 teaspoons
- Sugar - 0.5 teaspoons
- Flax seeds - 1 tablespoon
- Cranberry Dried - 1 tablespoon
- Vegetable oil - 1,5 tablespoons
- Soda - 1 teaspoon (incomplete)

**Preparation:**
1. Serum warm slightly, stir in it salt and sugar. Add whey, soda, seeds and butter to the flour. With a fork, knead the dough.
2. Add dried cranberries, mix the dough well, cover with food wrap, and let the test ripen for 30 minutes.
3. Lubricate your hands with vegetable oil. The dough should be well kneaded, formed any desired loaf, put in a pan. It is better to sprinkle with flour.
4. Sprinkle bread top with flax seeds and flour lightly. Bake bread in the oven at 180 degrees 45-50 minutes.

# Banana Bread With Walnuts

**Ingredients:**
- Butter - 120 g
- Sugar - 200 g
- Egg of chicken - 2 pieces
- Banana - 500 g
- Wheat flour - 160-170 g
- Baking Powder - 1.5 teaspoons
- Cinnamon powder - 0.5-1 teaspoons
- Vanilla sugar - 10 g
- Walnut - 70 g
- Vegetable oil - 1 teaspoon

**Preparation:**
1. Combine the softened butter and sugar and beat for a few minutes with a mixer until smooth. Continue to beat the mixture, add 1 egg chicken and whisk the mixture 40-60 seconds. Then add the second chicken egg and whisk the mixture for another 1-2 minutes.
2. Cut 2 large ripe bananas with a fork until smooth and add egg, sugar and butter to the mixture.
3. Gradually mix the sifted wheat flour and baking powder into the mixture. Add the vanilla sugar, ground cinnamon.
4. In the finished dough carefully, cut into large pieces of walnuts.
5. Pour the dough into a baking dish lined with oil and lined with baking paper and gently flattens.
6. Place the dough in a preheated oven to 170 degrees and bake for 50-60 minutes.

# Bread At Leaven

**Ingredients:**
- Starter wheat active - 70 g
- Wheat flour - 240 g
- Flour rye - 240 g
- Salt - 12 g
- Honey - 2 tablespoons
- Cumin seeds - 1 teaspoon
- Coriander seeds - 1 teaspoon

**Preparation:**
1. In the bowl mixer lay out the leaven, add water, salt, honey, both types of flour, spices. We knead the dough (nozzle - hook) for 15 minutes, hands - 20 minutes.
2. Cover the bowl with a film and leave it at room temperature for 12-14 hours.
3. Put the dough in a greased form. Cover the dough with a film and put it in a warm place for 1.5-3 hours.
4. Bake in a preheated to 200 degrees oven for 10 minutes with steam (at the bottom we put a couple of ice cubes), then reduce the temperature to 180 degrees and bake for another 40 minutes.

# Bread From Green Buckwheat

**Ingredients:**
- Green buckwheat - 400 g
- Brine - 200 ml

**Preparation:**
1. We will rinse the buckwheat and fill it with water, leave it for 2-3 hours for swelling.
2. After draining the water, buckwheat became soft.
3. Next, grind the green buckwheat with a blender; you need to achieve a homogeneous mass.
4. We connect buckwheat mass with brine, mix well.
5. We leave the dough from buckwheat in a warm place, cover with a towel, we wait. A natural fermentation process should occur, and this can take about 20 hours (maybe even more). To speed up the process, you can add a little baking soda.
6. Transfer the dough to a greased form. Bake bread at 190 degrees for about an hour.

# Armenian Bread

**Ingredients:**
- Flour, wheat - 400 g
- Water - 1 glass
- Fresh Yeast - 1/3 teaspoons
- Salt - 1/2 teaspoons
- Sugar - 1 teaspoon.
- Vegetable oil - 2 tablespoons
- sesame - to taste
- Chicken Yolk (optional)

**Preparation:**
1. We will shake the yeast in a bowl. We dilute with water at room temperature. A little sugar. Add the main amount of sifted flour. Next, vegetable oil and salt. Knead the dough.
2. Cover the dough with a food film. Then a towel. Remove the bowl in a warm place for 1.5 hours.
3. Cover the baking sheet with baking paper. We grease the leaf with vegetable oil. Place the dough in the middle of the pan. Press it with your hands, forming an oval cake. In the central part of flat cakes fingers need to press the ring.
4. Cover the workpiece with food film. Let's leave for a while.
5. Lubricate the bread with choleric. Lubricate the surface of bread with sesame.
6. Send to a well-heated oven for 20 minutes. Heating temperature - not less than 220 ° C. We bake the Armenian bread until golden brown.

# Sour Bread

**Ingredients:**
- Sugar - 1 teaspoon
- Yeast dry - 1 teaspoon
- Water at room temperature - 200 ml
- Wheat Flour - 200 g
- The whole
- Sugar - 1 tablespoon
- Salt - 1 teaspoon
- The water is warm - 100 ml
- Wheat Flour - 200 g
- Refined sunflower oil - 2 tablespoons

**Preparation:**
1. So, we mix all the constituents of the pits. Spoon a sticky dough. Cover the bowl with an opaque film and put it in the refrigerator for 12 hours.
2. We spread the scoop in the bowl of the mixer; add to it the other components. The flour must be sieved 3-4 times. We knead soft, but sufficiently sticky dough.
3. Put the dough in a bowl, oiled. Cover with a film and put in a warm place for 1.5-2 hours.
4. Put it in a greased form. Cover the film and leave in a warm place for another forty minutes.
5. Bake the bread in a preheated 200-degree oven for about 40 minutes.

# Brewed Bread

**Ingredients:**
- Flour - 360 g
- Milk - 240 ml
- Sugar - 1 tablespoon
- Salt - 1,5 teaspoons
- Yeast dry - 1 teaspoon

**Preparation:**
1. Prepare the tea leaves: pour 120 ml of milk into a saucepan or a small saucepan, send to a fire and bring to a boil. Pour 40 grams of wheat flour. Quick movements with a spoon all mix well until smooth. Pour the saucepan from the fire and cool it to a warm state.
2. In the bowl, pour the remaining milk, it should be warm. Add sugar and yeast. Stir and leave for 10 minutes.
3. The flour that remains, sift and add to the spatter. Pour in the salt. Slightly stir. Add the cooled tea leaves and start mixing everything thoroughly.
4. Put the dough in a bowl, greased with vegetable oil, cover with a towel and leave in a warm place for 2 hours. After 1 hour, the dough should be gently crumpled and sent on to rest.
5. Lubricate the baking dish with vegetable oil and lay out the dough, cover with a towel and leave in the heat for 30-40 minutes.
6. Bake the brewed bread in a preheated oven for 35-40 minutes at a temperature of 180 degrees.

# Banana Bread

**Ingredients:**
- Dry yeast - 5 g
- Milk - 200 ml
- Sugar - 1 tablespoon
- Salt - 1 teaspoon
- Banana - 1 piece
- Refined sunflower oil - 20 ml
- Wheat flour - 480 g
- Yolk 1 egg
- Milk - 1 tablespoon

**Preparation:**
1. Mix the flour with yeast, salt and sugar. Add warm milk and a forked banana pulp.
2. We knead the soft elastic dough. Spread it in a bowl, oiled. Cover the film and leave in a warm place for 1 hour.
3. Blow it up and form buns. We will cover with a towel and let's rest for 20-30 minutes.
4. Lubricate each bun with egg yolk mixed with milk. Bake in a preheated 180 degree oven for 20-30 minutes.

# Bread In A Slow Cooker

**Ingredients:**
- Whole wheat flour - 300 g
- Wheat flour - 200 g
- Sunflower kernels - 50 g
- Water - 150 ml
- Milk - 150 ml
- Sugar - 1 tablespoon
- Salt - 1 teaspoon
- Dry fast-acting yeast - 7 g
- Vegetable oil - 2 tablespoons
- Honey - 1 teaspoon

**Preparation:**
1. In a bowl we combine the following ingredients: whole-grain flour, part of sifted wheat flour (about 2/3), salt, sugar, yeast, and sunflower kernels. Mix to homogeneity.
2. Dissolve honey in milk. It is better to use liquid in this case.
3. In the center of the flour mix we make a so-called well and pour in liquid. Spoon begins kneading the dough.
4. Next we pour in the vegetable oil. Mix again.
5. Sift the remaining flour and proceed to manual kneading (5-10 minutes).
6. We form a ball from the dough, put it into a bowl, greased with vegetable oil, sprinkle with flour, and cover with a towel and leave it for 1 hour in a warm place.
7. We spread the dough on the table, sprinkled with flour, and as it should be kneaded it, again we form the ball. We transfer to the oiled bowl of the slow cooker, set the "Heating" mode for 20 minutes.
8. Set the "Baking" mode for 30 minutes. Then, using the steam stand, carefully take out half-finished breads and turn it over the other side. Stove on the other side for another 30 minutes.

9. Let the ready-made bread cool down with the lid open for 10 minutes.

# Filling Bread

**Ingredients:**
- Wheat Flour - 300 g
- Water - 350 ml
- Dry yeast - 6 g
- Sugar - 1 tablespoon
- Salt - 1 teaspoon

**Preparation:**
1. Pour sugar and yeast into warm water. Stir and leave for 10 minutes. Add salt and sifted flour. Use a spoon to knead the dough. The dough should be homogeneous and sticky.
2. Cover the bowl with a towel and leave in a warm place for 30 minutes.
3. Stir the dough and leave for another 30 minutes.
4. Cover the baking sheet with parchment and pour the dough.
5. Let him stand in the heat for another 10 minutes.
6. To send in the preheated to 200 degrees oven for 35-40 minutes. Bake jellied bread until ruddy.

# Unheated Bread In A Slow Cooker

**Ingredients:**
- Wholemeal flour - 2 cups
- Buckwheat flour - 1 glass
- Oat flour - 1 glass
- Water - 2 cups
- Chia seeds - 1/3 cup
- Flax seeds - 1 tablespoon
- Seeds of cumin - 1 tablespoon
- Coriander seeds - 1 tablespoon
- Honey - 2 tablespoons
- Mustard oil - 2 tablespoons
- Baking Powder - 1 tablespoon

**Preparation:**
1. Combine in a deep bowl of whole-grain flour, buckwheat and oatmeal. Mix. Add the baking powder and mix again. Pour warm water, honey and mustard oil. Stir thoroughly the whole mass.
2. Pour the seeds of chia, cumin, coriander and flax. Mix everything again.
3. Put it in a bowl, cover with a food film and leave to rest for about 20 minutes.
4. Put the dough on the table and give it the desired shape. Top grease with warm sweet water and sprinkle with seeds cumin, coriander and flax.
5. Bake unleavened bread for 120 minutes.

# Bread Without Yeast

**Ingredients:**
- Wheat flour - 400-480 g
- Baking Powder - 15 g
- Salt - 5 g
- Sugar - 40 g
- Butter - 80 g
- Light Beer - 330 ml

**Preparation:**
1. Mix the sifted flour, salt, sugar and baking powder. Pour the beer and mix well.
2. Lay it in a form, covered with parchment.
3. Melt butter, let it cool down a bit, and then pour over the dough. Bake in preheated to 190 degrees oven for about an hour.

# French Bread

**Ingredients:**
- Wheat Flour Extra Class - 340 g
- Salt - 7 g
- Dry quick-dissolving yeast - 3.5 g
- Water - 225 g

**Preparation:**
1. Combine the flour and dry instant yeast. Add the salt. Stir the ingredients.
2. Add a trickle of warm water.
3. Knead first with a fork, periodically wetting it in water. We leave the dough for 5 minutes, let it rest, and then knead it with your hands for about 2 minutes, until homogeneity.
4. On the working surface of the table, pour a little flour, spread the dough and knead it well for about 1 minute with your hands. Pour a larger saucepan with vegetable oil and put the cooked dough there. We put it in the refrigerator, covered with a film or a tight lid, for the night.
5. Oven should be heated up to 260 ° C 45 minutes before baking. Put an empty sheet on the bottom of the oven. Before baking, open the bread in 15 minutes and let it breathe. When we decided to bake, we take out the dough, cut it into rolls or baguettes, make cuts, sprinkle with water.
6. Gently put the bread on a baking sheet and put in a prepared oven for 30-35 minutes. After 12 minutes, reduce the temperature to 230 degrees. Prepare the French bread in the oven until the rolls become rosy-golden.

# Bread In A Slow Cooker

**Ingredients:**
- Wheat flour - 2 tablespoons
- Bran - 2 tablespoons
- Eggs - 2 pieces
- Baking Powder - 0.5 teaspoons
- Salt - 1 pinch
- Vegetable oil - 1 teaspoon
- Spices - to taste

**Preparation:**
1. Stir in the bowl of eggs. Add to them vegetable oil, flour with a baking powder and bran. Add spices to taste. Mix the ingredients together.
2. The dough turns liquid; it needs to be poured into a suitable greased form or silicone. The shape is chosen so that the height of the dough in it is about 3 cm.
3. Bake bread in a slow cooker for 7-8 minutes at a power of 600 watts.

# Bread "Pita"

**Ingredients:**
- Wheat Flour - 250 g
- Fresh yeast - 8 g
- Water (warm) - 125 ml
- Butter - 25 g
- Salt - 0.5 teaspoons

**Preparation:**
1. Pour the flour into the bowl, add salt. Dissolve the yeast in water and pour it into the flour. Add soft oil.
2. Knead the dough. Remove for ascent to heat.
3. Divide the dough into 6 equal parts. Roll each piece into a flat cake.
4. Put the tortillas on the baking tray with paper. Cover with a towel and leave for 15 minutes.
5. Heat the oven to 250 degrees. Bake for 6-7 minutes.

# Gray Bread

**Ingredients:**
- Flour, wheat 1 grade - 250 g
- Flour rye - 125 g
- Yeast, pressed - 13 g
- Water (warm) - 250 ml
- Sugar - 1 teaspoon
- Honey - 1 teaspoon
- Salt - 10 g
- Malt rye - 0,5-1 teaspoons
- Butter (soft) - 5 g

**Preparation:**
1. In a small bowl pour 50 ml of warm water, pour sugar and stir until it dissolves. Add the yeast, stir.
2. In another bowl, spread honey, salt and soft oil, pour the remaining (200 ml) warm water, mix.
3. In a suitable bowl, mix the first grade flour (150 g), rye flour (60 g) and malt.
4. We pour the resulting honey-and-oil mixture into the flour, mix it.
5. Get a viscous mass. We close both bowls with a towel and put them in a warm place for half an hour.
6. After half an hour we connect the contents of two bowls, gradually pour the remaining flour: 1st grade and rye. Knead the dough.
7. From the dough form the ball, put it on a baking sheet covered with baking paper. From above with a sharp knife we will make some cuts and we will put in flour. We cover with a towel and we clean for an hour and a half in a warm place.
8. Bake bread in the oven preheated to 220 degrees for the first 10 minutes with the steam (on the bottom of the oven put the container with hot water). After 10 minutes, we remove the

container with water. Reduce the temperature to 180. Continue baking the bread for 30-40 minutes.

# Bread In The Oven

**Ingredients:**
- Milk - 200 ml
- Butter - 35 g
- Yeast, pressed - 18 g
- Sugar - 1 tablespoon
- Salt - 1 teaspoon
- Flour, wheat - 400 g

**Preparation:**
Melt the butter in hot milk. Add the yeast to the bowl, allow them to completely dissolve. Pour out the flour, salt and sugar. Knead the dough. Cover and put in heat for lifting.
2. Shape a little oil for bread and sprinkle with flour. Put the dough in the mold. Cover and let the dough rise.
3. Bake bread on pressed yeast in the oven at a temperature of 180 degrees to a crispy crust. About 20 minutes.

# Whole-Grain Bread In The Oven

**Ingredients:**
- Wheat wholemeal flour - 550 g
- Water - 300 ml
- Dry yeast - 8 g
- Olive oil - 3 tablespoons
- Sugar - 1 tablespoon
- Salt - to taste

**Preparation:**
1. Sift 1/3 of whole-grain flour to sift several times. Then pour in the yeast and sift along with the flour. Pour in water at room temperature, add sugar and mix. Cover with a napkin and leave in a warm place for 15-20 minutes.
2. Then pour in the salt and pour in the olive oil. In parts, add sifted flour. Knead the dough. Pour a tablespoon of olive oil to it and continue to mix for 5 minutes.
3. Put it in a deep bowl and cover with a napkin. Leave in a warm place for 25-30 minutes. After that, again, thoroughly rewind and roll into a ball.
4. Put the workpiece in a greased baking dish, cover with a napkin and leave for 15 minutes.
5. Then, if desired, sprinkle flour and make shallow incisions with a sharp knife. Then send it to the oven.
6. Bake bread in the oven for 25-35 minutes at a temperature of 200 degrees.

# Whole-Wheat Bread On Kefir

**Ingredients:**
- Kefir 2,5% - 400 ml
- Dry yeast - 10 g
- Salt - to taste
- Olive oil - 2 tablespoons
- Wholemeal flour - 550 g

**Preparation:**
1. Sift 1/3 of the flour two or three times. At the time of sifting, add dry yeast. Then pour in warm kefir and mix the mass thoroughly. Cover with a napkin and leave for 15 minutes in a warm place.
2. Pour the salt to taste and start pouring the flour into pieces. It is also necessary to sift, and better - 2-3 times. After each addition of flour you need to carefully, but slowly, to mix.
3. Pour a tablespoon of olive oil and continue to mix for another 5-7 minutes. Put it in a deep bowl, cover with a napkin and leave in a warm place for 25-35 minutes.
4. Then mix it again, form a loaf and put it in a greased form. Cover with a napkin and leave for 10-15 minutes.
5. Bake at 220 degrees for 10 minutes, then reduce the temperature to 200 and continue baking for another 15-20 minutes.

# Bread On Mashed Potatoes

**Ingredients:**
- Mashed potatoes - 200 g
- Milk - 160 ml
- Sugar - 40 g
- Dry yeast - 7 g
- Butter - 70 g
- Salt - 1 teaspoon
- Wheat flour - 450 g
- Yolk 1 egg
- Milk - 1 tablespoon

**Preparation:**
1. Preparing the sponge. Milk, sugar, salt, butter, put in a bucket, heat, so that the butter melted. Add the mashed potatoes to this mixture and stir well with a whisk so that there are no lumps. Add 150 g of flour and yeast to this mixture. Mix well.
2. Cover with a film and leave in a warm place for 20-30 minutes.
3. Gradually add the remaining flour into it and knead the soft elastic dough.
4. Put the dough in a bowl, oiled. Cover the film and leave in a warm place for 1 hour.
5. We put the bread on the baking tray, cover it with a towel, let it stand for about 30 minutes, then grease it with yolk and milk.
6. Bake bread in the oven heated to 200 degrees for 20-25 minutes.

# Wheat-Rye Bread In The Oven

## Ingredients:
- Wheat Flour - 300 g
- Rye flour - 150 g
- Malt rye fermented - 1 teaspoon
- Dry yeast - 7 g
- Salt - 0.5 teaspoon
- Honey - 1 teaspoon
- Water 250 ml

## Preparation:
1. Mix both kinds of flour, yeast, malt and salt. Add warm water and honey. We knead the dough, which we put into a bowl, oiled. Cover the film and leave in a warm place for 30-40 minutes.
2. We spread it on the working surface, we knead it. We form the loaf (or bowl), put it on a baking sheet covered with parchment or oiled. Cover the towel and leave in a warm place for 30 minutes.
3. After half an hour, we grease the bread with water, sprinkle with flour, and make a sharp incision with a sharp knife.
4. We send the bread in a preheated oven to 250 degrees (put a bowl of water on the bottom of the oven or put a few ice cubes - this will be steam). Bake in the oven for 20 minutes, and then reduce the temperature to 200 degrees and bake for another 30 minutes.

# Round Bread

**Ingredients:**
- Dry yeast - 4 g
- Salt - 1 teaspoon
- Sugar - 1 teaspoon
- Wheat flour - 320 g
- Water - 200 ml
- Refined sunflower oil - 30 ml

**Preparation:**
1. Mix flour, salt, sugar and yeast. Add warm water and oil. We knead the dough. Spread it in a bowl, oiled. Cover the film and leave in a warm place for 40-50 minutes.
2. We spread it on the working surface, we knead it. We form a ball, which we spread on a baking sheet, covered with parchment or oiled. Cover the towel and leave in a warm place for 30-40 minutes.
3. We make arbitrary cuts. We send the baking tray with bread in a preheated oven to 200 degrees for 25-35 minutes.

# Grain Bread

**Ingredients:**
- Milk - 250 ml
- Sour cream - 100 g
- Egg - 1 piece
- Salt - 2 g
- Butter - 60 g
- Dry yeast - 10 g
- Flour, wheat - 400 g
- Pumpkin seeds - 70 g
- Seeds of sunflower - 30 g
- Flax seeds - 30 g
- Sesame - 10 g

**Preparation:**
1. In a deep bowl, pour the milk at room temperature. Pour in the dry yeast. Pour 2 tablespoons of sifted flour. Stir, cover with a napkin and set aside in a warm place for 15 minutes.
2. When the opara rises to lay out to it sour cream, chicken egg, salt and butter. Mix the mass until uniform. And introduce 2/3 sifted flour. Pour pumpkin seeds, sunflower seeds, and flax and sesame seeds. Stir and add the remaining flour.
3. Lay baking dish with baking paper or grease with vegetable oil. Put the dough and flatten the top of the product. Top with a mixture of seeds.
4. Cover the form with a napkin and leave in a warm place for 20-30 minutes. Then send it to the oven.
5. Bake bread in the oven for 25-30 minutes at a temperature of 180-200 degrees.

# Bread By Dyukan

**Ingredients:**
- Cottage cheese fat-free - 125 g
- Egg of chicken - 2 pieces
- Salt - 1 pinch
- Oat bran - 4 tablespoons
- Wheat bran - 2 tablespoons
- Baking Powder - 1 teaspoon
- Sesame - 1 pinch (optional)

**Preparation:**
1. Chop the cottage cheese to a homogeneous pasty state.
2. Connect 2 eggs with 1 pinch of salt and whip with a fork until smooth.
3. Mix the egg mixture and cottage cheese. Add oatmeal, wheat bran and baking powder. Thoroughly mix everything.
4. Fix the baking sheet with baking paper and grease with a small amount of vegetable oil.
5. Put the prepared dough in the mold, if desired; sprinkle the surface of the dough with a pinch of sesame.
6. Place the bread in the oven, preheated to 180 degrees, and bake for 25-30 minutes, until golden brown.

# Bread On Kefir On Yeast

**Ingredients:**
- Kefir 250 ml
- Wheat Flour - 450-500 g
- Yeast dry - 1 teaspoon
- Salt - 1 teaspoon
- Sugar - 1 teaspoon
- Egg - 1 piece

**Preparation:**
1. Kefir needs to be slightly warmed up, add sugar, yeast and 30 g of flour from the total amount. Stir the opar and leave it in the heat for 20 minutes. In the egg, separate the yolk, add it to the spoon and mix well.
2. Then add salt and half the remaining flour. Stir the dough. Then gradually pour the remaining flour and knead the soft dough.
3. Cover the bowl with the dough and put it in a warm place for 2 hours.
4. Then dough the dough again and place it in a parchment-covered form. Give the test to rise again in the form. Form a loaf and put it on a baking sheet. The test will take about 30 minutes. After that, loosen the top of the bread with a lightly whipped protein.
5. Heat the oven to 180 degrees and bake bread for 30-35 minutes.

# Bread On Kefir In A Bread Maker

**Ingredients:**
- Wheat Flour - 550 g
- Yeast, fresh - 20 g
- Kefir 250 ml
- Water - 50 ml
- Vegetable oil - 1,5 tablespoons
- Butter - 20 g
- Egg of chicken - 1 piece
- Sugar - 1 tablespoon
- Salt is small - 1,5 tablespoons

**Preparation:**
1. Dissolve the yeast in warm water.
2. According to the instructions, load all the ingredients in the bowl.
3. Bake bread on kefir in the bread maker in the "Basic" or "White bread" mode, weight - 1 kg, crust - medium.

# Wheat Bread With Rye Starter

**Ingredients:**
- Rye starter - 1 glass
- Wheat flour - 2 cups
- Warm water - 1 glass
- Salt - 0.5 teaspoons
- Sugar - 1 teaspoon
- Vegetable oil

**Preparation:**
1. Pour the rye ferment into a deep container, fill the warm water with a temperature of no more than 30 C, pour in salt and sugar, and mix thoroughly.
2. Put the sifted wheat flour in pieces and knead the dough.
3. If desired, you can add spicy herbs to the dough.
4. Lubricate with a vegetable oil baking dish or parchment paper. Put the dough there and cover with a towel. Place in a warm place and let rise about 25-30 minutes. Then put the form in the oven at 200 C for 40-45 minutes.

# Onion Bread In The Oven

**Ingredients:**
- Flour, wheat - 400 g
- Warm water - 1 glass
- Yeast - 1 teaspoon
- Sugar - 1 tablespoon
- Salt - 0.5 teaspoons
- Olive oil - 4 tablespoons
- Onion - 1 piece

**Preparation:**
1. Yeast dilute in warm water, add sugar. Leave the minutes for 10 minutes.
2. On a quiet fire in a minimum amount of vegetable oil fry the onion until golden brown, cool.
3. Add the sifted flour, olive oil and salt to the yeast. Add a little water, start kneading the dough.
4. Add the fried onions, continue to knead the dough. Cover the dough with food wrap and put in a warm place for 30-40 minutes.
5. After a while, the dough should be well kneaded. Form the bread baking grease with vegetable oil or lined with baking paper, put the dough, cover with a clean kitchen towel and give another 20 minutes to come.
6. Bake in preheated to 220 degrees oven for the first 10 minutes, and then reduces the temperature to 180 degrees and bake for another 40-50 minutes.

# Quick Bread In The Oven

**Ingredients:**
- Flour - 500-550 g
- Milk (warm) - 300 ml
- Dry quick-acting yeast - 6 g
- Vegetable oil (refined) - 20 ml
- Egg - 1 piece
- Salt - 1 teaspoon
- Honey - 20 g

**Preparation:**
1. In a container with warm milk, we introduce salt, egg and honey, and mix it with a handful of whisk.
2. We pour in the vegetable oil. Fast dry yeast is mixed with sifted flour and gradually poured into a container with liquid ingredients. Knead the dough.
3. Put the dough into a bowl and mix it with a hand mixer for 4-5 minutes.
4. Leave the dough in a warm place for 5-10 minutes, covered with a towel.
5. Then transfer the dough into the form (23x9 cm). The form is pre-covered with baking paper; we apply sidewalls with margarine or oil. We cover the top with a towel and put it away in a warm place for 30-40 minutes.
6. Put the form in a preheated to 180-190 degrees oven and cook for 25-35 minutes.

# Bread With Dry Yeast In A Slow Cooker

**Ingredients:**
- Flour wheaten (w / s) - 850 g
- Dry quick-acting yeast - 15 g
- Sugar - 30 g
- Salt - 10 g
- Water (room temperature) - 500 ml
- Vegetable oil - 40 ml

**Preparation:**
1. In a bowl with a handful of whisk we mix the sifted flour, sugar, salt and fast-acting yeast.
2. In the flour mix, make a groove in the center and with a thin trickle pour in water, first mix it with a spoon, and then - with hands.
3. Then pour in vegetable oil and continue to knead the dough.
4. As soon as the butter completely intervenes in the dough, we spread it on the table and knead it to elasticity.
5. We put a bowl of a slow plate with oil; we spread dough into it. Close the lid. We turn on the "Bread" program, set the time to 3 hours and press the "Start" button.
6. 60 minutes before the end of the program, open the lid, and using a bowl for steaming, turn the bread. If there is no such bowl, you can use a plate or a towel. Close the lid and cook the bread until the end of the program.

# Amaranth Bread

**Ingredients:**
- Flour wheat whole-grain - 350-400 g
- Flour amaranth - 100 g
- Dry yeast - 5 g
- Sugar
- Salt
- Milk - 320 ml
- Refined sunflower oil - 20 ml

**Preparation:**
1. In a bowl of a mixer (or a bowl) we pour amaranth flour, we will add yeast and milk. Stir well. Cover with a film and leave in a warm place for 20-30 minutes.
2. Add salt, sugar, sunflower oil. Then, pouring wheat whole-grain flour, knead the soft elastic dough.
3. Put it in a bowl, oiled. Cover the film and send it to a warm place for 1-1.5 hours with a wake in 40-50 minutes.
4. After the required time, we knead the dough, form bread. We spread it on a baking sheet, covered with parchment, cover it with a towel and leave it in a warm place for 30-40 minutes.
5. Bake bread in the preheated oven to 220 degrees for the first 10 minutes with steam (put a bowl of boiling water on the bottom of the oven). Then the temperature is reduced to 180 degrees and we bake the bread for another 30-40 minutes.

# Wheat-Rye Bread In The Bread Maker

**Ingredients:**
- Water - 240 ml
- Vegetable oil - 2 tablespoons
- Salt - 1,5 teaspoons
- Rye flour - 140 g
- Wheat flour - 280 g
- Yeast dry - 1.5 teaspoons

**Preparation:**
1. For bread weighing 750 g, it is necessary to combine the products in the bowl of the bread maker in the following sequence: pour 240 ml of water, add 2 tablespoons (22 g) of vegetable oil, pour 1.5 teaspoons (9 g) of salt, then pour 140 g of sifted rye flour and wheat flour - 280 g.
2. Add 1.5 teaspoons (9 g) of dry yeast to the flour.
3. Shape with all the ingredients put in the bread maker. Close the lid and connect the bread maker to the mains.
4. Choose a program for wheat-rye bread. The time for baking such bread in the bread maker is 4 hours. After the sound signal, turn off the bread maker from the mains, open the lid and get the finished bread.

# Homemade Wheat Bread In The Oven

**Ingredients:**
- Dry yeast - 5 g
- Wheat Flour - 380-400 g
- Sugar - 2 tablespoons
- Salt - 1 teaspoon
- Water - 240 ml
- Olive oil - 30 ml

**Preparation:**
1. Preparing the sponge. From the total amount of flour, take 5 tablespoons of flour, mix with yeast, and add water. Mix well. Cover the film and leave in a warm place for 20-30 minutes.
2. We introduce sugar, salt, olive oil. Add the flour. We knead the dough, which we put into a bowl, oiled. Cover the film and leave in a warm place for 1 hour.
3. We knead the dough, form the loaf, and put it into a form covered with parchment. You can lubricate with oil, and then parchment is not used. We'll cover with a towel and let's stand still for 40 minutes.
4. Bake the bread in the oven, heated to 200 degrees, 10 minutes, then lower the temperature to 180 degrees and bake for another 20-30 minutes.

# Whole-Grain Bread Without Yeast In The Oven

**Ingredients:**
- Rye sourdough - 30 g
- Wholemeal flour - 400 g
- Wheat Flour - 200 g
- Salt - 10 g

**Preparation:**
1. Make the spit. We take the necessary amount of active rye ferment, mix it with water and whole-grain flour. Mix well. Cover the jar with a lid and leave it at room temperature for 12-16 hours.
2. Put the whole spoon in the bowl, add water. Then - two kinds of flour and salt. Mix the dough for 10 minutes in a stationary mixer or 15 minutes with your hands.
3. We spread the dough into a bowl, greased with oil, cover with a film and leave in a warm place for 2-3 hours.
4. Denounce it. We put in any form for baking, oiled. We cover with a film and again we leave in a warm place for 1,5-2 hours.
5. We spread it on a baking sheet covered with parchment; we make incisions with a sharp knife. Bake in the oven, heated to 220-230 degrees, 40-45 minutes. The first 10 minutes - with the steam (at the bottom of the oven you should put a bowl of boiling water or throw a few ice cubes). After 10 minutes, a bowl of boiling water is removed.

# Bread "Taba-Nan"

**Ingredients:**
- Water - 125 ml
- Milk - 125 ml
- Flour, wheat - 400 g
- Yeast, fresh - 20 g
- Salt - 0.5 teaspoons
- Sugar - 0.5 teaspoons
- Vegetable oil - 1 tablespoon

**Preparation:**
1. Milk and water should be slightly heated. Dissolve yeast and sugar in the liquid. Pour out the flour and salt. Stir and then add oil at the end. Carefully knead the dough.
2. Cover the dough and put it in the heat for lifting. It is advisable to dough a couple of times.
3. Divide the dough in half. With your hands, form a cake with edges from the dough.
4. Transfer the blanks to the baking sheet. Bake in a hot oven at 200 degrees to a rosy color. Approximately 12-15 minutes.

# English Muffin Rolls

**Ingredients:**
- Wheat Flour - 150 g
- Dry yeast - 5 g
- Salt - 0.5 teaspoons
- Sugar - 1 teaspoon
- Milk - 100 ml
- Butter - 40 g

**Preparation:**
1. Mix the flour with yeast, salt and sugar. Milk warm and melt the butter. Pour all into a dry mixture. Stir the dough with a spoon. Cover and remove in heat for 15-20 minutes.
2. Lubricate the cupcake mold. Spoon the dough. Bake English muffin rolls at a temperature of 180 degrees to a crispy crust, 15-20 minutes.

# Norwegian Grain Breads

**Ingredients:**
- Flour, wholemeal - 200 g
- Oatmeal / oat flakes - 200 g
- Sunflower seeds - 100 g
- Flax - 50 g
- Sesame - 50 g
- Salt - 0.5 teaspoons
- Sugar / honey - 1 teaspoon (optional)
- Carbonated / Drinking Water - 700 ml
- Vegetable oil - 1 tablespoon

**Preparation:**
1. Connect the whole-grain flour and ground (or whole) oat flakes of instant cooking. Add sunflower seeds, flax and sesame seeds, salt and a little sugar or honey, if desired. Mix everything well. Pour in water at room temperature.
2. Mix the ingredients and allow the mass to infuse for 10-15 minutes.
3. Line the baking tray with baking paper and oil with vegetable oil. Spread half the dough and evenly distribute a thin layer.
4. Using the dough knife, cut the mass into rectangles of the desired size. If desired, sprinkle the surface of the dough with a small amount of seeds, for decoration.
5. Place the dough in a preheated oven for 170-175 degrees and bake for 40-45 minutes. Then reduce the heat to 160 degrees and cook the loaves for another 15-25 minutes.
6. Divide the finished loaves, completely cool and place in a sealed storage container. Repeat the procedure with the remaining test.

# Roll With Poppy Seeds

**Ingredients:**
- Wheat Flour - 500 g
- Dry yeast - 4 g
- Salt - 7 g
- Sugar - 18 g
- Honey - 10 g
- Butter - 10 g
- Water - 280-290 ml
- Poppy - for sprinkling

**Preparation:**
1. Mix flour, salt, sugar, honey, yeast, butter and water. We knead the soft elastic dough.
2. We form a ball from the test. We spread it on a plate, sprinkled with flour. Cover the towel and let the test stand for 30 minutes.
3. Lay it on the work surface. Form the oval. We wrap one edge, then the second one. And turn off the roll. We spread the roll into a bowl, oiled, and covered with a film and leave with a warm place for 2.5-3 hours. During this time we knead the dough 2 times: after 40 minutes and after an hour and a half.
4. After 2,5-3 hours the dough is divided into 2 parts, from each we form the loaf. We put the blanks on a baking sheet covered with parchment. Let the loaves settle for 1.5 hours.
5. Sprinkle the loaves with water, sprinkle abundantly with poppy seeds and sprinkle again with water. We bake a loaf with poppy seeds in a 200-degree oven heated for 30 minutes.

# Buns With Garlic

**Ingredients:**
- Milk - 200 ml
- Sugar - 1/2 tablespoons
- Butter - 40 g
- Egg - 2 pieces
- Dry yeast - 8 g
- Salt - to taste
- Flour - 400 g
- Garlic - 1 head
- Greenery (dill, parsley) - 1 bundle
- Vegetable oil - 50 ml

**Preparation:**
1. In a deep bowl, pour in the milk of room temperature; add sugar, dry yeast and 2-3 tablespoons of sifted flour. Stir and leave under a napkin in a warm place for 15-20 minutes.
2. When the opara is ready, pour in the melted butter, two chicken eggs and salt. Stir everything to homogeneity and start to add flour in parts. When the dough absorbs all the flour, continue to knead another 5-10 minutes.
3. Cover the dough with a damp cloth and leave for 1.5-2 hours for the approach.
4. The dough must be kneaded and divided into several parts for convenience in further work. From each part alternately roll the roller, and in its turn divided into small parts.
5. Each of them is rolled between two hands in a ball and put in a greased form, leaving a small distance between the balls. Cover the form with a napkin and leave to approach for 20 minutes in a warm place.
6. Then send to the oven and bake for 25-30 minutes at a temperature of 180 degrees.

7. Prepare the sauce: in a deep bowl squeeze garlic cloves garlic, pour finely chopped greens, salt and pour in vegetable oil. Mix everything.

8. Gently remove the buns from the mold. Divide them and put them into prepared sauce. Stir so that each bun is well wrapped in garlic sauce.

# Whole-Wheat Loaves With Bran On Kefir

**Ingredients:**
- Wheat Flour - 230 g
- Wholemeal flour - 230 g
- Dry yeast - 6 g
- Refined sunflower oil - 3 tablespoons
- Sugar - 2 tablespoons
- Salt - 1.5 teaspoons
- Kefir - 200 ml
- Water - 170 ml
- Bran - 3 tablespoons

**Preparation:**
1. Mix both kinds of flour, yeast, bran, salt and sugar. Add warm water and kefir, sunflower oil. We knead the soft elastic dough.
2. Put it in a bowl, oiled. Cover with a film and put in a warm place for 1 hour.
3. We spread the dough on the working surface, divide it into 2 parts. From each part we form a loaf. We put the blanks on a baking sheet covered with parchment, cover with a towel and put the baking sheet in a warm place for 30 minutes.
4. Lightly sprinkle them with flour, and cut them with a sharp knife. We send it to the preheated oven to 210 degrees for 30-40 minutes.

# Chocolate Bun

**Ingredients:**
- Milk - 250 ml
- Fresh yeast - 25 g
- Wheat Flour - 500 g
- Sugar - 150 g
- Cocoa powder - 40 g
- Egg - 1 piece
- Butter - 50 g
- Salt - pinch
- Vanillin - 1 g
- Candied fruits - 2 handfuls
- Vegetable oil

**Preparation:**
1. In a bowl, pour warm milk, add 20 g of sugar from the total mass and crush the yeast. Remove to a warm place and wait until the yeast has risen.
2. In a separate container to sift the flour and cocoa, add vanillin and salt. Melt and cool the butter, mix with the spelled and add to the dry mixture.
3. Separately beat the egg. In the dough, add sugar and enter the egg. Stir first with a spatula, and then continue kneading your hands.
4. When the dough begins to lag behind the sides of the bowl, add the candied fruit.
5. Collect the dough into a bowl. Lubricate the bowl with vegetable oil, put the dough, cover with a towel and clean for 1 hour in a warm place.
6. Divide the dough into pieces and spread it into molds to half, and cover the sides with parchment. Leave for another 1 hour, so that the dough rises in the forms.
7. Heat the oven to 180 degrees and bake chocolate cakes for about 35 minutes.

# The Custard Cake

**Ingredients:**
- Milk - 300 ml
- Wheat Flour - 900 g
- Vanilla - 1 pod
- Yeast, fresh - 15 g
- Eggs - 5 pieces
- Butter - 200 g
- Vegetable oil - 50 ml
- Cranberry jelly - 50 g

**Preparation:**
1. Warm up a little 100 ml of milk, crush yeast, and add salt and 100 g of flour. Leave for lifting.
2. Pour the remaining milk into a saucepan and bring to a boil, remove from heat. Cut the vanilla pod, scrape the seeds and put them in the milk, and drop the vanilla pod. Cover the pan for 10 minutes.
3. During this time, sift 150 g of flour into a separate bowl. Then remove the vanilla pod from the milk, again bring the milk to a boil, pour all the flour immediately and remove from heat. Knead the mass to homogeneity.
4. During this time, the opar will do. In the bowl, shift the brewed dough, add to it the spoon, mix and leave for 1 hour in a warm place.
5. The next step is to separate the proteins from the yolks. Proteins to clean for a while in the refrigerator, and put the yolks in a bowl and add sugar.
6. Beat the mass with a mixer until the yolks turn white.
7. In the dough, add the yolks with sugar, add another 150 grams of sifted flour, carefully mix the whole mass and again put it in a warm place for 1.5 hours.

8. After this time, melt the butter and cool a little. In the dough pieces add the remaining flour and pour oil. Thoroughly knead the dough.

9. At the end of the mix, add whipped proteins and vegetable oil to the dough. After the dough becomes homogeneous, sprinkle it with a little flour and add the dried fruits.

10. Once again knead the dough well. Dilute the dough into molds. The test is given to rise in the forms to the very top or slightly higher, while baking it will still rise.

11. Heat the oven to 180 degrees and bake the custard cakes 30-35 minutes.

# Cottage Cheese Cake Without Yeast

**Ingredients:**
- Curd soft home - 300 g
- Wheat Flour - 500 g
- Eggs - 2 pieces
- Sugar - 180 g
- Milk - 100 ml
- Vegetable oil - 4 tablespoons
- Vanillin - 1 g
- Soda - 1 teaspoon
- Salt - 0.5 teaspoons
- Cranberry jelly - 100 g
- Lemon or lime juice - 1 teaspoon

**Preparation:**
1. In a bowl, break the eggs, add sugar and salt. Beat the whisk to a uniformity. Add in the egg mass vegetable oil, barely warm milk and slaked soda. Soda can be extinguished with lemon or lime juice. Also add the cottage cheese and grind the whole mass well.
2. Then add to the dough washed and slightly steamed raisins or candied fruit.
3. Sift the flour into the dough and add vanillin (1 g) or vanilla sugar (10 g). First, stir the dough with a spoon, then with your hands until it gathers into a bowl.
4. The forms are covered with parchment. Dough put on half the forms.
5. Bake in a preheated 180 degree oven for about 1 hour.

# Homemade Bread

**Ingredients:**
- Flour - 3 cups
- Salt - 1 teaspoon
- Sugar - 2 teaspoons
- Dry quick-acting yeast - 1 teaspoon
- Vegetable oil - 1 tablespoon
- Milk powder - 2 tablespoons
- Water - 220 ml

**Preparation:**
1. Pour warm water into the bowl of the bread maker.
2. Pour the water on the flour, salt, sugar, yeast, milk powder and vegetable oil. We include the program "Admixtures of yeast dough". The program is mixed for 1 hour and 50 minutes.
3. After a specified time, we put the grown dough on the table. We form a loaf of bread.
4. We shift the bread into the bowl of the bread maker, from which it is necessary to remove the kneading levers first. We make several cuts on the bread with scissors.
5. Turn on the oven for 50 degrees, cover the bowl with a towel and send it for 20 minutes in the oven.
6. After a set time, take out the bread; raise the temperature to 180 degrees. Remove the towel from the bread and send the cup to the oven for 35-45 minutes.

# Bread With Spinach

**Ingredients:**
- Bread mixture - 0,5 kg
- Spinach frozen - about 100 g
- Water - 200 ml
- Vegetable oil - 1 tablespoon
- Dry active yeast - 1,5 teaspoons

**Preparation:**
1. Defrost the spinach at room temperature, and preferably in a microwave at low power. Pour about 200 ml of water to the spinach.
2. In the form of the bread maker on the blade for the knife, pour in the oil, set the knife to knead the dough and pour the spinach water. Then add the bread mixture and top dry active yeast.
3. Set the mode of "white bread", the desired color of crust, weight 750 g and in the first minutes of kneading, watch for the formation of "bread".

# Bread With Bran In A Bread Maker

**Ingredients:**
- Flour - 350 g
- Rye flour - 150 g
- Water or serum - 300 ml
- Vegetable oil - 1 tablespoon
- Bran - from 2 tablespoons
- Yeast - 1.5 teaspoons
- Sugar - 2 teaspoons
- Salt - 1 teaspoon
- Dry aromatic herbs and spices - to taste

**Preparation:**
1. I recommend first to pour a serving of vegetable oil on a knife pin, and then install it and pour in water (or whey). Dry fragrant herbs can be added immediately, let them get wet in the liquid.
2. Send salt to the breadmaker's form, both kinds of flour, sugar and bran.
3. Lastly put the yeast on top.
4. Set the mode for bread from wholemeal or whole-grain flour, weight 750 g and the desired color of the crust and the first minutes follow the formation of the dough ball from the dough. If necessary, correct it with flour or water.

# Thin Focaccia On Ricotta

**Ingredients:**
- Wheat Flour - 200 g
- Ricotta cheese - 100 g
- Garlic - 1 tooth
- Oregano - 1 teaspoon
- Yeast, fresh - 12 g
- Milk - 50 ml
- Sugar - 0.5 teaspoons
- Olive oil - 3 tablespoons
- Salt - 0.5 teaspoons

**Preparation:**
1. Dissolve the yeast in warm milk. Add sugar, flour, ricotta, oregano, garlic and salt passed through the press. Knead the dough and leave for 30 minutes.
2. Put the dough on a baking sheet with parchment, form a focaccia oval shape, make small grooves with fingers and sprinkle with olive oil.
3. Bake in a 220-degree preheated oven for 20 minutes.

# Whole-Grain Bread With Acetane

**Ingredients:**
- Wheat Flour - 250 g
- Wholemeal flour - 150 g
- Water 250 ml
- Milk powder (or substitute) - 2 tablespoons
- Vegetable oil - 1 tablespoon
- Yeast dry - 1 teaspoon
- Acetan - 1.5 teaspoons
- Sugar - 0,5 tablespoons
- Salt - 0.5-1 teaspoons
- Cereals and seeds - up to 1 cup

**Preparation:**
1. Connect water with vegetable oil, milk powder and salt. Add both types of flour, sugar, yeast and acetan.
2. Set the mode for the yeast dough and in the first minutes look after the formation of the kolobok. You may need to adjust the dough with flour or water.
3. After the sound signal, add the grain part (seeds, flakes ...).
4. Put the dough into the mold or on the baking tray after two of its lifts. Let the dough come up again for 15-25 minutes.
5. Then place in a preheated oven and bake at 180-200 degrees for about an hour.

# Focaccia With Fried Onions And Cheese

**Ingredients:**
- Water - 180 ml
- Dry yeast - 5 g
- Honey - 1 teaspoon
- Salt - 0.5 teaspoons
- Wheat flour - 280 g
- Olive oil (vegetable) - 2.5 tablespoons
- Cheese - 50 g
- Onion - 1 piece

**Preparation:**
1. Add honey and yeast to warm water. Add salt. In portions, pour out the flour, knead the dough. At the end, add oil (1.5 tablespoons). Cover and put in a warm place for lifting.
2. Peel onion and finely chop. Fry with the addition of oil.
3. When the dough increases in volume, cut into cubes cheese.
4. Add cheese and onions to the dough. Stir well.
5. Shape the form with oil. Put the dough, level, finger to make holes throughout the test. Lubricate the cake with butter. Cover and let it go up a bit.
6. Sprinkle the cake with herbs. Bake at a temperature of 180 degrees to a rosy color, about 20 minutes.

# White Bread On Sunflower Oil

**Ingredients:**
- Dry yeast - 6 g
- Flour, wheat - 400 g
- Salt - 1 teaspoon
- Sugar - 20 g
- Water - 240 ml
- Refined sunflower oil - 40 ml

**Preparation:**
1. From the total amount of flour we measure 120 grams and mix it with warm water and yeast. We mix everything well. Cover the film and leave in a warm place for 15-20 minutes. It will be an opara.
2. We pour oil into it; add sugar, salt and flour.
3. Mix the soft elastic dough, which we put in a bowl, oiled. Cover the film and leave in a warm place for 1 hour.
4. We embed it, form the loaf, which we put in a form, oiled or covered with parchment. Cover the towel and leave in a warm place for 30 minutes.
5. Bake in a preheated 200 degrees oven for 15 minutes, and then reduce the temperature to 180 degrees and bake for another 20-30 minutes.

# Australian Unleavened Bread

**Ingredients:**
- Self-rising flour - 450 g
- Olive oil - 1 tablespoon
- The water is warm - 225-250 ml
- Salt - 0.5 teaspoons
- Rosemary - 3 sprigs
- Olives - 1 pot

**Preparation:**
1. Sift the flour and make a deepening in the center. To make this bread, use self-rising flour. Next, pour in the olive oil. Add salt, warm water and chopped rosemary.
2. Mix the ingredients and knead for a few minutes until homogeneous dough is obtained.
3. Flatten the dough, giving it the shape of a flat bun. In the center place the sliced olives. Collecting dough from the edges to the center, knead the dough for a few more minutes to mix and evenly distribute the filling.
4. Send the bread in a preheated oven to 180-200 degrees and bake for 30-35 minutes.

# Toast Bread

**Ingredients:**
- Milk - 200 ml
- Butter - 50 g
- Yeast dry - 1.5 teaspoons
- Sugar-1 tablespoon
- Salt - 1 teaspoon
- Wheat Flour - 370 g

**Preparation:**
1. To prepare the dough in warm milk, pour out the sugar and yeast. Leave for 5 minutes. Add salt and soft oil. Pour out most of the flour, mix with spatula.
2. After pouring the remaining flour, knead the dough with your hands. Cover the dough with a towel and remove to rise in a warm place.
3. Lubricate the bread pan with butter. Form the bread in shape, cover and leave to rise.
4. Put the form in a preheated oven, the temperature is 180 degrees, until golden brown, about 20 minutes.

# Bread From Baking Mixture

**Ingredients:**
- Wheat Flour - 250 g
- Bread mixture - 250 g
- Dry yeast - 5 g
- Salt - 10 g
- Water - 260 ml

**Preparation:**
1. Pour water, and then fill all the dry ingredients in the bucket bread maker. We put it into the oven and select the "bread" program.
2. When there is a signal, the program is completed and the bucket can be removed.

# Classic Homemade Borodino Bread In The Oven

**Ingredients:**
- Wheat Flour - 170 g
- Rye flour - 300 g
- Dry yeast - 3 g
- Refined sunflower oil - 2 tablespoons
- Water 400 ml
- Rye malt - 2 tablespoons
- Salt - 1 teaspoon
- Honey - 1 tablespoon
- Coriander dry - to taste

**Preparation:**
1. Brew the malt. Fill the malt with 150 ml of boiling water, stir. We put it aside, let it cool down a little.
2. The remaining 250 ml of water is mixed with honey. Mix both kinds of flour, yeast; add salt, dissolved in water malt and water with honey. We will add oil there.
3. Mix the soft dough. We spread it in a bowl, greased with sunflower oil. Cover with a film and leave in a warm place for 1-1,5 hours.
4. We embed it, put it in a form, oiled or lined with parchment. Lightly water, sprinkle coriander, lightly pressing it into the dough. Cover the towel and leave in the warmth for 30-40 minutes.
5. Bake the bread in a preheated 180 degree oven for about 40 minutes.

# Focaccia With Cherry And Provencal Herbs

**Ingredients:**
- Dry yeast - 5 g
- Wheat flour - 450 g
- Salt - 1 teaspoon
- Sugar - 1 tablespoon
- Butter - 20 g
- Olive oil - 70 ml
- Water - 220 ml
- Cherry tomatoes - to taste
- A mixture of Italian herbs - to taste

**Preparation:**
1. Mix flour, salt, sugar, yeast. Add warm water, softened butter and olive oil.
2. We knead the soft elastic dough. Spread it in a bowl, oiled. Cover the film and leave in a warm place for 1 hour.
3. We embed it; put it in a form lined with parchment. Cherry tomatoes cut into 2 parts, spread them on the dough, slightly pressing. Top with sprinkled with herbs.
4. Bake in preheated to 210 degrees oven for about 30 minutes.

# Bread On Kefir With Mustard And Mayonnaise

**Ingredients:**
- Kefir - 300 ml
- Flour - 400 g
- Mayonnaise - 4 tablespoons
- Mustard - 1 teaspoon
- Salt
- Sugar
- Yeast, fresh - 10 g
- Sesame - if desired

**Preparation:**
1. In the lukewarm kefir we add mustard, salt, sugar, yeast and mayonnaise. All mixed and gradually add flour. Knead the dough.
2. The dough is covered with a food film and leave for 60 minutes to approach in a warm place.
3. Then divide the dough into two equal parts.
4. Cover the parchment with parchment. From each piece of dough to form a ball. Put them on a baking tray and top out the cuts. Sprinkle bread on top with flour or sesame. Leave it once again to go for 30 minutes.
5. Bake bread in a preheated oven at a temperature of 200 degrees 30 minutes.

# Bread On Kefir Without Yeast

**Ingredients:**
- Flour - 300 g + for mixing
- Kefir - 300 ml
- Salt - 1 teaspoon
- Sugar - 1 teaspoon
- Soda - 0.5 teaspoons

**Preparation:**
1. Put salt and sugar in the flour. We mix. Half a teaspoon of soda is quenched with a teaspoon of kefir. We put soda in the flour and add the remaining kefir.
2. Pour in the flour and knead the soft dough.
3. Dough wraps in food film and leave for 30-40 minutes to dough rested. We form round bread from the dough. We make cuts from above. Sprinkle bread with a small amount of flour.
4. Preheat oven to 220 degrees and put baking bread for 50 minutes. After 25 minutes, reduce the temperature to 200 degrees.

# Italian Bread

**Ingredients:**
- Sugar - 1 tablespoon
- Yeast dry - 1.5 teaspoons
- Wheat flour - 450 g
- Milk - 125 ml
- Butter - 100 g
- Milk - 125 ml
- Salt - 1 teaspoon

**Preparation:**
1. Mix the yeast with flour (100g) and sugar. Pour warm milk, stir. Cover and remove to heat until the opara rises.
2. Add the milk, soft oil, salt and remaining flour to the spoon. Knead soft elastic dough. Cover and remove the fit. Rinse once and again to come up.
3. Divide the dough into 2 parts. Each roll into a rectangle. Each rectangle is divided into 8 parts. Dipping a piece of dough into the melted butter, put it in a bread mold.
4. Cover for 5-10 minutes. Bake Italian bread at a temperature of 200-220 degrees until cooked, about 30-40 minutes.

# Whole-Grain Buns

**Ingredients:**
- Wholemeal flour - 500 g
- Water - 300 ml
- Yeast, fresh - 15 g
- Olive oil - 1 tablespoon
- Salt - 0.5 teaspoons

**Preparation:**
1. Dissolve the yeast in 50 ml of warm water. Add flour, olive oil, salt, remaining water and knead the dough for 10 minutes.
2. Form the ball and leave for 30 minutes in a warm place.
3. Approached the dough to crumple and divide into 4 parts. Roll each piece of dough into a rectangle, and then fold to the center twice along the long side and traverse the rolling pin.
4. And then roll up the roll. Thus, to form 4 rolls, put on a baking sheet with parchment and leave for 1 hour.
5. Bake in preheated to 190 degrees oven for 20-25 minutes.

# Apple Bread On Mayonnaise

**Ingredients:**
- Water - 120 ml
- Mayonnaise - 50 g
- Sugar - 1 teaspoon
- Salt - 0.5 teaspoons
- Apple - 0,5 pieces
- Dry yeast - 5 g
- Wheat Flour - 330 g

**Preparation:**
1. We will peel the apple and peel it on a fine grater. Heat the water so that it is warm, but not hot, add mayonnaise, grated apple. We mix it.
2. In another bowl, sift flour; add yeast, salt and sugar. We connect both mixtures.
3. Mix the soft elastic dough. We spread it into a bowl, oiled with oil, cover with a film and leave it in a warm place. After an hour, we cheat and leave for another hour.
4. We form a loaf, put it in a form, oiled or paved with parchment. Cover with a towel and leave for 30 minutes.
5. Bake in a preheated 180 degree oven for about 40 minutes.

# Oatmeal Bread In The Bread Maker

**Ingredients:**
- Wheat Flour - 390 g
- Oatmeal flakes - 120 g
- Pig fat - 30 grams
- Whey Milk - 300 ml
- Salt - 2 teaspoons
- Sugar - 2 tablespoons
- Milk powder - 1.5 tablespoons
- Yeast dry - 1.5 teaspoons

**Preparation:**
1. Pour the whey into a bucket of bread and add the melted fat. To fall asleep oat flakes.
2. Sift the flour into a bucket, sprinkle powdered milk, sugar and salt in the corners. In the center, pour in the yeast, making a small hole.
3. Set the main mode, weight 1 kg, medium crust.

# Homemade Loaf On Kefir

**Ingredients:**
- Kefir - 2 cups
- Flour - 4 cups
- Honey - 1 tablespoon
- Yeast, fresh - 10 g
- Salt - 0.5 teaspoons
- Sesame - 1 tablespoon
- Egg - 1 piece

**Preparation:**
1. In kefir room temperature add salt, honey and yeast. Stir well and pour in a portion of the flour. Knead the dough, cover with a towel and put in a warm place for an hour and a half.
2. When the dough is good, roll it up with an oval.
3. Cover the pan with parchment paper. Cut the dough with a roll and put on a baking tray. At the top of the loaf make slashes, grease with a beaten egg and sprinkle with sesame.
4. Bake the loaf in a preheated oven at 200 degrees for 30 minutes.

# Viennese Baguettes

**Ingredients:**
- Yeast, fresh - 10 g
- Butter - 30 g
- Flour - 1,5 cups
- Salt - pinch
- Sugar - 1 tablespoon
- Milk - 175 ml
- Sesame - 0.5 tablespoons

**Preparation:**
1. In a little warm milk put yeast, salt, sugar and pour melted butter. It is good to mix everything and add gradually the flour, which must first be sifted.
2. Knead the soft dough. Cover the dough with a towel and leave in a warm place for an hour.
3. When the dough has come, divide it into 4 parts. Each piece of dough rolled length of about 30 cm, and a width of 12-15 cm.
4. Roll out a piece of dough, roll up. Make a baking sheet with baking paper and lay out baguettes on it. On the baguettes make oblique incisions. And leave them again a little bit to go, about 30 minutes.
5. When the baguettes are a little bit approached, grease them with milk and sprinkle with sesame seeds.
6. Baguettes are baked in a preheated oven, at a temperature of 180 degrees, for 12-15 minutes.

# Baton Is Portioned

**Ingredients:**
- Wheat Flour - 250 g
- Yeast dry - 1 teaspoon
- Butter - 30 g
- Milk - 180 ml
- Salt - 1 teaspoon
- Sugar - 1 teaspoon

**Preparation:**
1. Dissolve yeast and sugar in warm milk. Add melted butter, flour and salt. Knead the dough. Leave for lifting.
2. Divide the dough into three equal parts. Roll the dough into a thin layer, approximate width 15 cm, length 30 cm.
3. Twist the roll, turn the edges. Transfer the loaves to the baking tray, cover with a towel and leave for 15 minutes.
4. Cut with a sharp knife and smear with milk.
5. Bake at a temperature of 180-200 degrees to a rosy color.

# Dough For Tartlets

**Ingredients:**
- Wheat Flour - 225 g
- Butter - 150 g
- Egg large SW - 1 piece
- Salt - 1 teaspoon

**Preparation:**
1. Mix the softened oil and egg with a spatula. Sift to an oily-egg mixture with flour and salt.
2. Knead the soft and elastic dough. The dough should be kneaded quickly for 5-8 minutes.
3. Dough for tartlets and snack baskets is ready.

# Wheat Home Noodles

**Ingredients:**
- Flour - 350 g
- Eggs of chicken - 5 pieces
- Salt - 1 teaspoon

**Preparation:**
1. We sift the flour and 2/3 of the part is poured into a deep bowl. We drive five pieces of chicken eggs, add salt and begin to knead the dough.
2. First, a little spoon, connect the eggs with flour, and then we dump the mass on the flour-strewn table. And we start to collect the dough in a heap, that is, knead it. We do not add water. Gradually, if necessary, add the rest of the flour.
3. Ready the dough to roll into a bowl and pack it in a food film or in a plastic bag. Dough must rest for at least an hour.
4. From the finished test cut a small piece, roll it into a ball. The table is sprinkled with flour and we begin to roll this piece into a thin layer.
5. Roll the layer on the towel and leave to dry for 10-15 minutes, and we roll the next cake ourselves.
6. Slightly dried cake is rolled into a tube and cut into rings. The width of the noodles is also made at will.
7. After that, homemade wheat noodles can be cooked or folded in bags and stored in the freezer.

# Cake With Sour Cream With Candied Fruit

**Ingredients:**
- Sour Cream - 0,5 cups
- Flour - 2,5-3 cups
- Milk - 1/3 cup
- Eggs - 2 pieces
- Sugar - 0,5 cups
- Butter - 50 g
- Yeast dry - 1 teaspoon
- Candied fruit - 1-2 handfuls
- Vanilla sugar - to taste
- Citrus peel - optional
- Salt - 1 pinch

**Preparation:**
1. Warm the milk until warm with butter, mix.
2. Stir eggs with salt. Combine the milk mass with egg, with sour cream and with sugar. Stir.
3. Add flour, preferably sifted, and dry yeast. Knead the dough and add the candied fruit.
4. Give the dough once to rise, dock it, several times knock on the table, and then divide into portions suitable for the size of the molds, if you do not bake in one big one. The portion of the dough should be about 1/3 of the height of the mold.
5. When the dough already in the forms will rise significantly - by 2/3 of the height of the mold, it's time to send it to a preheated oven. Bake cakes at 180-200 degrees until cooked. Finished cakes decorate with icing, sweetening and sprinkling.

# Fast Cake In The Bread Maker

**Ingredients:**
- Yeast dry - 2.5 teaspoons
- Flour - 400 g
- Milk - 170 ml
- Sugar - 5 tablespoons
- Salt - 1/2 teaspoons
- Butter - 2 tablespoons
- Eggs - 3 pieces
- Vanilla sugar - 1 packet
- Dried cranberries - 100 g

**Preparation:**
1. Milk should be warm, and the rest of the ingredients are at room temperature, the flour must be sifted.
2. Put the ingredients in the bucket in the right order. Pour yeast, flour, sugar, salt, vanilla sugar into a bucket. Drive eggs and add soft butter. Pour in the milk. Then add cranberries.
3. Bake on the "Fast" basic mode. Size - M, color of crust - medium. If desired, decorate with icing or sprinkle with powdered sugar.

# Easter Cottage Cheese Cake

**Ingredients:**
- Cottage cheese - 150 g
- Milk - 100 ml
- Vegetable oil - 50 ml
- Egg - 1 piece
- Sugar - 4-5 tablespoons
- Vanilla sugar - 1-2 teaspoons
- Raisins - 1 handful
- Wheat flour - 300 g / 2.5 cups
- Baking Powder - 1.5 teaspoons

**Preparation:**
1. Mix cottage cheese, egg, sugar, milk and vegetable oil. Then add the flour with the baking powder. Stir and knead soft, lush dough.
2. Wash the raisins and, if necessary, if it is dry, then steam it off. Stir raisins into the dough.
3. Place the dough in a suitable size or in one shape so that it occupies 2/3 of the volume.
4. Bake cottage cheese cakes in the oven at 180 degrees until cooked for 30 to 45 minutes. If desired, decorate with icing or sprinkle with powdered sugar.

# Roman Focaccia

**Ingredients:**
- Wheat flour - 4 tablespoons
- Mineral water - 80 ml
- Salt - 1 teaspoon
- Sugar - 2 teaspoons
- Dry yeast - 3 g
- Flour - 330 g
- Mineral water - 190 ml
- Salt sea - 2 pinch

**Preparation:**
1. Mix flour, salt, sugar and yeast, fill with mineral water. Good mix. Cover the film and leave it at room temperature for 20 minutes.
2. In a bowl or in a container for a mixer, we sift the flour; add all the spit and the remaining mineral water.
3. Mix the soft dough. When the dough is collected in a sure lump, add the olive oil. And again we mix, that the oil is completely absorbed into the dough.
4. Put the dough in a bowl, oiled. Cover the film and put it in a warm place for 1.5 hours.
5. Spread it on the work surface, divide into 2 parts. From each we form 2 flat cakes 1-1.5 cm thick each. Fingers make grooves, grease with olive oil, and sprinkle with sea salt.
6. Bake in a preheated 230 degree oven for 15-20 minutes.

# Wheat Bread In A Breadmaker

**Ingredients:**
- Milk - 150 ml
- Water - 140 ml
- Wheat Flour - 500 g
- Yeast dry - 1.5 teaspoons
- Sugar - 1,5 tablespoons
- Salt - 1,5 teaspoons
- Sunflower oil - 1,5 tablespoons
- Dill dry - 1-2 tablespoons
- Garlic seasoning - 1 teaspoon

**Preparation:**
1. Pour warm water and milk into the bucket of the bread maker, pour in the sunflower oil. Gradually sift all the flour.
2. In the corners, sprinkle salt, sugar, dry dill and garlic seasoning. In the center make a hole and pour in the yeast.
3. Set the main mode, bread weight - 750 g, the color of the crust can be selected light or medium. For an average crust it will take 3 hours 25 minutes.

# Burrito With Rice

**Ingredients:**
- Rice color - 60 g
- Sunflower seeds (brushed) - 100 g
- Honey - 5 teaspoons
- Yeast dough - 500 g
- Vegetable oil - 100 ml

**Preparation:**
1. From 500 grams of yeast dough should be 10 biscuits with rice. Therefore, I divide the dough into 10 parts of 50 grams.
2. The rice must be boiled beforehand until ready. Lay out ready-made rice and 10 grams of peeled seeds for each piece of dough.
3. Close the cake as a patty, gently connecting the edges to the center. And roll out a rolling pin a thin cake no more than 5 mm thick.
4. In a frying pan, heat the vegetable oil and put the cake with rice. Fry from both sides and put in a dish. While the cake is hot, it should be smeared with honey.

# Wheat Starter For Bread

**Ingredients:**
- Wheat Flour - 150 g
- Flour rye - 100 g
- Water 75 g
- Honey - 1 teaspoon

**Preparation:**
1. In the morning. In a clean dry jar we pour wheat flour - 100 grams. Add rye flour - 50 grams, water - 75 grams and honey - 1 teaspoon. Stirring.
2. Cover with gauze or cloth, intensively letting air in and put in a warm place for 36-48 hours.
3. Next, we take half the leaven (and unfortunately we throw it away). The rest is fed: add wheat flour - 50 grams, rye flour - 25 grams, water - 75 grams.
4. Stir, cover and again put in a warm place.
5. Again, take half of the leaven and re-feed: wheat flour - 50 grams, rye flour - 25 grams, water - 75 grams.
6. The next stage begins for 3 to 4 days. Twice a day, in the morning and in the evening, we take part of the leaven, leaving 75 g in the can. We divorce 75 g of water and add 75 g of flour (50 g of wheat flour and 25 g of rye).
7. Continue feeding every 12 hours, but now only with wheat flour: take half and add 75 g of wheat flour and 75 ml of water.
8. The leaven will increase in volume, and somewhere on the 6-7th day you can consider it ripe. From such ferment you can bake bread.

# Unleavened Bread In The Oven

**Ingredients:**
- Kefir - 350-400 ml
- Flour - 450 g
- Soda - 1 teaspoon
- Salt - 1 teaspoon
- Sugar - at will
- Spices - to taste

**Preparation:**
1. Mix both kinds of flour with soda and salt. Pour in kefir. First mix the mass with a spatula. Then quickly knead the dough and collect it into a bowl.
2. Transfer the dough to a greased baking sheet or mold. Make a knife cut the top of the bread crosswise.
3. Place the bread in a preheated 200 degree oven and bake for about 45 minutes.

# Mustard Bread

**Ingredients:**
- Wheat Flour - 400 grams
- Water - 230 ml
- Sugar - 1,5 teaspoons
- Salt - 1 teaspoon
- Mustard powder - 1,5 tablespoons
- Dry yeast - 4 grams
- Refined sunflower oil - 3 tablespoons
- Egg - 1 piece
- Milk - 2 tablespoons
- Sesame - if desired

**Preparation:**
1. Mix flour, salt, sugar, mustard powder and yeast. We pour warm water.
2. Knead soft elastic dough. We spread the dough into a bowl, greased with sunflower oil. Cover the film and leave in a warm place for 1.5 hours.
3. We embed it; put it into a baking dish. Cover the towel and leave in a warm place for 30-40 minutes.
4. Lubricate a loaf of eggs mixed with milk. Sprinkle with sesame seeds (optional). Bake in a preheated oven to 200 degrees for about 30 minutes.

# Leaven For Unleavened Bread

**Ingredients:**
- Wheat Flour - 300 grams
- Water - 300 ml

**Preparation:**
1. Connect in a convenient container 100 grams of flour and 100 ml of warm water.
2. Mix the flour with water to the consistency of sour cream. Cover the dishes with leaven of gauze and leave for a day in a warm place.
3. After a day, the leaven was covered with a crust, and inside it formed bubbles. Add again 100 ml of water and flour 100 grams. All mix and leave for another day.
4. On the second day, repeat the same actions. On the third day the leaven is ready.

# Dough For Homemade Noodles

**Ingredients:**
- Wheat Flour Extra Class - 180 grams
- Flour wheaten from a flour of firm grades - 100 gram
- Eggs large chicken - 2 pieces
- Salt - 1 teaspoon

**Preparation:**
1. Mix both kinds of flour in a bowl. In the middle, make a hollow and beat the eggs in there. Add the salt. Start kneading the dough. When it becomes difficult to interfere with the spatula, start kneading the dough with your hands.
2. As a result, you should get smooth and elastic dough of a yellowish hue.
3. Dough for homemade noodles is ready.

# White Bread In The Oven

**Ingredients:**
- Wheat flour - 800-850 grams
- Yeast dry - 1 teaspoon
- Sugar - 1 tablespoon
- Salt - 1,5 teaspoons
- Kefir or sour milk - 1 glass
- Water - 1 glass
- Egg - 1 piece

**Preparation:**
1. Mix the yogurt and water in a bowl. Water should be heated, so that all the liquid was warm. Add the sugar and yeast and leave the yeast to work.
2. Pour 2-3 glasses of flour into a bowl, mix the dough with a spatula.
3. Then gradually add the rest of the flour, thoroughly stirring. Finished dough is sprinkled with flour and left for 1 hour in a warm place, covering the bowl with a lid.
4. Divide the dough into two equal parts and form a round loaf of each. Cover the baking sheet with parchment and lay the dough at a distance from each other. Lubricate with beaten egg. Bread left for another hour for lifting.
5. Then heat the oven to 200 degrees and bake bread for 25-30 minutes.

# Bread With Rye Bran

**Ingredients:**
- Yeast dry - 1 teaspoon
- Water - 230 ml
- Honey - 1 tablespoon
- Salt - 1 teaspoon
- Rye bran - 4 tablespoons
- Olive oil - 20 ml
- Wheat Flour - 380 grams

**Preparation:**
1. Mix the flour with salt, yeast and rye bran. We warm the water so that it is warm. Put honey in it; stir it, so that the honey is completely dissolved. Add the mixture to the flour.
2. Knead the soft dough. Once it is collected in a ball, add the olive oil and continue to mix. In total it will take about 10 minutes.
3. Put the dough in a bowl, oiled. Cover the film and leave in a warm place for 1.5 hours.
4. We spread it on the work surface, we knead it. We form a bun, which we put on a baking sheet covered with parchment. Cover the towel and leave for 30 minutes.
5. We'll sprinkle it with flour and a sharp knife. Bake in preheated to 200 degrees oven for about 40 minutes.

# Bread With Matcha Tea

**Ingredients:**
- Water - 240 ml
- Yeast dry - 7 grams
- Flour - 400 grams
- Olive oil - 40 ml
- Sugar - 2 teaspoons
- Salt - 1 teaspoon
- Match Tea - 1 teaspoon

**Preparation:**
1. Mix the warm water with yeast and 120 grams of flour. Let's stand up. Then add the oil, salt, sugar.
2. Divide the mixture into 2 parts and add the Matcha tea to one. Then add flour to each part. We knead the dough.
3. Put the dough for lifting. We will divide it in a cup in a package. Divide the finished dough into an equal number of koloboks.
4. We put them in the form in checkerboard order. Form the paper, lubricate with oil. And we set still to rise.
5. When the dough is suitable, put in a preheated oven for 15 minutes at a temperature of 200 degrees.

# Dough Dumplings In A Breadmaker

**Ingredients:**
- Wheat Flour - 480 grams
- Egg of chicken - 1 piece
- Water - 210 ml
- Salt - 1 teaspoon
- Vegetable oil refined - 2 tablespoons

**Preparation:**
1. In the water, stir the egg and salt. Pour the liquid into the bowl of the bread maker and add the oil. Sift flour.
2. Set the bowl in the bread maker and select the "Fresh pastry" mode.
3. Close the dough in a bag and let it rest. After 25 - 30 minutes, the dough can be used.

# Bread Linz

**Ingredients:**
- Water - 200 ml
- Wheat Flour - 150 grams
- Rye flour - 150 grams
- Sugar - 1 tablespoon
- Salt - 1 teaspoon
- Egg of chicken - 1 piece
- Yeast dry - 7 grams
- Olive oil - 2 tablespoons

**Preparation:**
1. Mix both kinds of flour, yeast, salt, sugar. Add warm water, egg and olive oil. We knead slightly sticky dough and put it in a bowl, oiled. Cover the film and leave in a warm place for 30 minutes.
2. Drain it and put it back in a bowl, cover it with a film and leave it in a warm place again for 30 minutes.
3. Denounce it. We form the loaf and put it in a greased form. We will cover the form with a towel and give a rest for 20-30 minutes.
4. Bake in a preheated 180 degree oven for 1 hour.

# Egg Noodles

**Ingredients:**
- Eggs of chicken C1 - 3 pieces
- Water - 100 ml
- Salt - 1 teaspoon
- Wheat Flour - 480 grams

**Preparation:**
1. Pour the water into the bowl of the bread maker and add whipped eggs, salt. Sift flour. We set the bowl in the bread maker. Choose the mode «Unleavened dough for pasta" and press start.
2. We wrap the dough in a bag or food film and let it rest for 30 minutes.
3. Cut off part of the test. We dust the table with flour and roll out the dough thinly. All the dough is rolled out and laid out, so that it is slightly dried. We turn off the cakes. Finely cut into noodles.
4. Dry little noodles with flour. We leave to dry.

# Bread In Greek Yoghurt

**Ingredients:**
- Greek yoghurt - 120 ml
- Butter - 20 grams
- Salt - 1 teaspoon
- Sugar - 1,5 tablespoons
- Wheat Flour - 500 grams
- Water - 280 ml
- Yeast dry - 5 grams

**Preparation:**
1. Warm up the water, add butter and let it dissolve. There we add Greek yogurt, mix well.
2. In another bowl, mix the flour, salt, sugar, yeast. We combine both mixtures and knead soft dough, which we put into a bowl, oiled. Cover the film and leave in a warm place for 1 hour.
3. Spread it on the work surface and knead it. Spread out in a mold, oil it with oil. Cover the towel and let us rest for 20 minutes.
4. Bake in preheated to 190 degrees oven for about 40 minutes.

# Ukrainian Dumplings

**Ingredients:**
- Wheat flour - 3 cups
- Yeast dry - 3 teaspoons
- Water - 1 glass
- Honey - 1 tablespoon
- Sunflower oil - 3 tablespoons
- Garlic - 3 cloves
- Eggs - 1 piece
- Green parsley - 1 beam
- Salt - 1 teaspoon

**Preparation:**
1. Dry yeast mixed with honey and some water. The water should be warm.
2. In the sifted flour pour the yeast mixture, vegetable oil and add salt. Knead the dough, add it with a kolobok and leave for 15 minutes to rest.
3. The dough is a little bit approached, it needs to be kneaded, rolled balls of arbitrary size and put in a baking pan. The form can be oiled. Leave the dumplers for 30-40 minutes to go.
4. Lubricate them with beaten egg and put in the oven to bake. Bake in the oven at 200 degrees to a crispy brown.
5. While the dumplings are baked, cook the garlic grease: mix the crushed garlic squeezed through the press with 1 tablespoon vegetable oil, 1 tablespoon water and a pinch of salt. Chop the greens of parsley.
6. Lubricate hot Ukrainian dumplings with garlic mixture and put for another 5 minutes in the oven.

# Wheat-Rye Bread With Nuts

**Ingredients:**
- Yeast dry - 6 grams
- Nuts - 50 grams
- Wheat Flour - 350 grams
- Rye flour - 150 grams
- Water - 380 ml
- Sugar - 1 tablespoon
- Salt - 1,5 teaspoons

**Preparation:**
1. Nuts chop, to get pretty large pieces.
2. Mix two kinds of flour, yeast, salt, sugar, add crushed nuts and warm water. We knead soft, elastic dough. We spread it into a bowl, greased with sunflower oil, cover with a film and leave it at room temperature for 2 hours.
3. We spread it on the working surface, we knead it. We form the loaf, which we put on a baking sheet covered with parchment. Cover with a towel and leave at room temperature for 1 hour.
4. We will pour the loaf with flour, we will make incisions. Bake in a preheated to 220 degrees oven for 15-20 minutes, then reduce the temperature to 190 degrees and bake for another 25 minutes.

# Armenian Lavash

**Ingredients:**
- Wheat flour - 3 cups
- Water - 1 glass
- Salt - 0.5 teaspoons

**Preparation:**
1. In a deep bowl, falls asleep flour. We must sift the flour. We take hot water, we dilute salt in it. We make a groove in the flour and pour in water, gradually stirring the flour.
2. Then knead the dough. Ready, well-kneaded dough we put in a plastic bag can be wrapped in a food film or covered with an inverted bowl. Leave it for half an hour.
3. Make a sausage from the dough and divide it into equal pieces approximately the size of a chicken egg. Roll out the cake thinner.
4. Bake in a well-heated frying pan for two minutes on each side without oil.

# Buns "Roses"

**Ingredients:**
- Yeast dough - 800 grams
- Caramel Fruit - 200 grams
- Sugar - 2 tablespoons
- Egg of chicken - 1 piece
- Vegetable oil - 1 tablespoon

**Preparation:**
1. Divide the dough into small pieces. Roll the dough into circles 0.5 cm thick. Make 4 notches on the sides.
2. In the center, put caramel, 1 tablespoon of filling per 1 roll.
3. We wrap one of the four parts of the dough around the filling, as if casting on the filling, and fasten the bottom, at the bottom of the rolls, the same we do with the other "petals". Place of fastening should be as low as possible, at the bottom of the rolls.
4. We connect as tightly as possible, especially the last part.
5. We cover the baking tray with baking paper. We put out our roses and give the test 20 minutes. Then grease with a loose egg. Sprinkle the buns with sugar or cinnamon at will.
6. Bake in preheated oven at 180 degrees for 20-25 minutes.

# Bread Forming

**Ingredients:**
- Wheat flour - 600-650 grams
- Yeast dry - 1 teaspoon
- Kefir - 1 glass
- Water - 1 glass
- Sugar - 1 tablespoon
- Salt - 0.5 tablespoons
- Sesame - for sprinkling
- Egg - for lubrication

**Preparation:**
1. In a bowl, pour warm water and kefir, add sugar and yeast. Leave for 15 minutes until the yeast is blocked.
2. Sift in a bowl 500 g of flour and salt. Stir with spatula. Then pour more flour into the dough. Cover the bowl with the test towel and leave for 1 hour.
3. After an hour, add a little flour, knead the dough and roll the koloboks out of it, tearing it apart. Form a parchment and lay out chaotically all the koloboks. Leave the dough for another hour.
4. When the dough is suitable to grease the top of the bread with a beaten egg and sprinkle with sesame seeds as desired. You can use herbs or flax seeds.
5. Preheat oven to 200 degrees, put bread in it and oven for 20-25 minutes.

# Bread "Matnakash"

**Ingredients:**
- Wheat Flour - 250 g
- Water - 175 ml
- Yeast dry - 0.5 teaspoons
- Salt - 0.75 teaspoons
- Sugar - 0.25 teaspoons
- Sunflower oil - 1,5 tablespoons

**Preparation:**
1. Sift the wheat flour. Add dry yeast. Pour salt and sugar. We pour sunflower oil and warm water. Knead the soft dough. We knead minutes 15-20. We cover with a towel and leave in a warm place for 60 minutes.
2. Put the rest of the dough on a dust-laden board and leave it for 5 minutes. Carefully roll out into an oval, approximately 1-1.5 cm in thickness. We put it on a baking tray, cover it with a towel and leave it in a warm place for 30-40 minutes.
3. Fingers make grooves on the dough layer and send to the hot oven for 190-200 degrees for 30-35 minutes.

# Claret "Tempura"

**Ingredients:**
- Rice or wheat flour - 3 tablespoons
- Corn flour - 3 tablespoons
- Egg - 2 pieces
- Ice water
- Salt and spices - to taste

**Preparation:**
1. Stir eggs with ice water. Add flour and, if desired, baking powder.
2. Stir the mass manually with a fork or a whisk in a more or less homogeneous mass and the glue is ready.
3. Add salt and spices to it.
4. The "tempura" claret for use should be cold; sometimes even ice cubes are placed in it.

# White Bread In A Bread Maker

**Ingredients:**
- Wheat Flour Extra Class - 550 g
- Kefir - 300 ml
- Egg - 1 piece
- Sugar - 1 tablespoon
- Salt - 1 tablespoon
- Yeast dry - 2 teaspoons
- Butter - 20 g
- Sunflower oil - 1.5 tablespoons

**Preparation:**
1. Preheat kefir and pour it into the breadmaker's container. Add the melted butter, sunflower oil and beaten egg.
2. Sift the flour, pour sugar and salt into the corners. Sprinkle yeast in the center.
3. Install the program "Basic mode" in the bread maker, the bread weight is 1 kg, the crust is light.

# Bread From Wheat Flour With Honey

**Ingredients:**
- Milk - 300 ml
- Dry yeast - 6 g
- Honey - 20 g
- Sunflower oil - 30 g
- Salt - 10 g
- Wheat Flour - 500 g
- Yolk chicken - 1 piece
- Sesame black - 10 g

**Preparation:**
1. Pour the milk in a suitable container and warm it up a little. Pour warm milk into deep dishes. In milk, we dissolve honey, add dry yeast. Leave in a warm place for 10-15 minutes.
2. Pour salt, pour sunflower oil. Stir until the salt dissolves. Pre-sift, through a fine sieve, flour. We introduce small portions into the milk formula. Stir with a spoon.
3. As soon as the spoon becomes difficult to interfere, we spread the dough on the board, which we sprinkle with a little flour. We continue to knead with our hands.
4. The dough is placed in a deep dish, covered with a kitchen towel and left in a warm place, approximately, for 1 hour.
5. The rest of the dough is well kneaded on a dusty board. The form for baking is covered with parchment paper. We put our bread in shape. We cover with a towel and leave in a warm place for 30-40 minutes.
6. Lubricate with whipped egg yolk and sprinkle with sesame seeds. We send in the oven 180 degrees to a crispy crust.

# Baguettes With Whole Wheat Flour And Bran

**Ingredients:**
- Dry yeast - 8 grams
- Wheat Flour - 300 grams
- Wholemeal flour - 150 grams
- Salt - 1 teaspoon
- Honey - 1 tablespoon
- Water 250 ml
- Refined sunflower oil - 3 tablespoons
- Wheat bran - 4 tablespoons

**Preparation:**
1. Mix both kinds of flour, salt, yeast, wheat bran. Add warm water, honey and sunflower oil. We knead the soft elastic dough.
2. We put the dough in a bowl, greased with sunflower oil, cover with a film and leave it in a warm place for 1 hour.
3. Lay it on the work surface, divide into 2 parts. Each part is stretched in length, forming thin loaves. We put them on a baking sheet, covered with parchment and sprinkled with flour. Cover the towel and leave for 20-30 minutes.
4. We will sprinkle them with flour, we will make incisions. Bake in a preheated to 195 degree oven with steam for about 30 minutes. At the bottom of the oven put a container of water - it will be steam.

#  Part 2

# Introduction

When we talk about going on a diet or controlling your food intake, the first thing we are told is to cut out carbs, especially bread from our diet. This book is going to bust this myth and will show you how you can eat bread that is low carb and ketogenic diet-friendly.

The recipes mentioned in this book will not use white flour or all-purpose flour, which we all know offers zero nutrition and is high on bad carbs. Instead we have used healthier options like coconut flour and almond flour as a substitute, which is not just healthy but also helps makes tastier variants of breads.

These low carb breads are keto-compliant and can be used and consumed anytime while on a keto diet or even if you are not following a diet but want to eat healthier varieties of bread.

The ingredients mentioned in the book are commonly available and the recipes are extremely easy to follow. So without any further ado, let's get started.

Thanks again for purchasing this book. I hope you enjoy it!

# Chapter 1: Ketogenic Bread Recipes

## Low Carb Keto "Cornbread"

Serves: 12 slices

Nutritional values per serving:
Calories –193, Fat –16.3 g, Carbohydrates –2.8 g, Protein –2.1 g

Ingredients:

Dry ingredients:

- 2 cups almond flour
- 1 teaspoon salt
- 1 ½ teaspoons baking powder

Wet ingredients:

- 4 large eggs
- ½ cup full-fat sour cream
- 3-4 green onions, finely chopped
- 4 tablespoons butter

Method:

1. Add all the dry ingredients into a bowl.
2. Add all the wet ingredients into a large bowl. Whisk well.
3. Add the dry ingredients into the bowl of wet ingredients and mix well.
4. Pour into a greased loaf pan.
5. Bake in a preheated oven at 350º F for about 20-25 minutes or until light brown on top and the edges.

6. Cut into slices and serve.

# Cheese And Jalapeño Bread

Serves: 8 slices

Nutritional values per serving:
Calories –137, Fat –11 g, Carbohydrates –4 g, Protein –6 g

Ingredients:

Wet ingredients:

- 8 eggs
- ½ cup water
- ½ cup butter

Dry ingredients:

- 2/3 cup coconut flour
- 1 teaspoon garlic powder
- ½ teaspoon baking powder
- 1 teaspoon pepper powder
- 1 teaspoon salt

Other Ingredients:

- 1 cup cheddar cheese, grated
- ½ cup Parmesan cheese, grated
- 8 jalapeño chilies, deseeded, chopped

Method:

1. Add all the dry ingredients into a bowl.
2. Add all the wet ingredients into a large bowl. Whisk well.

3. Add the dry ingredients into the bowl of wet ingredients and mix well.
4. Add jalapeños, cheddar cheese and Parmesan cheese and stir.
5. Pour into a greased loaf pan that is also lined with parchment paper.
6. Bake in a preheated oven at 400º F for about 20-25 minutes or until light brown on top and the edges.
7. Cut into slices and serve.

# Keto Bread

Serves: 4 slices

Nutritional values per serving:
Calories –87.5, Fat –6.8 g, Carbohydrates –2.6 g, Protein –4.3 g

Ingredients:

- 3 large eggs, separated
- A pinch salt
- A pinch cream of tartar (optional)
- ¾ cup almond flour
- 1 ½ teaspoons baking powder
- 2 tablespoons butter

Method:
1. Add cream of tartar and egg whites into a mixing bowl. Beat until soft peaks are formed.
2. Add rest of the ingredients into the food processor bowl and pulse until the mixture is well combined. Add about ¼ of the beaten white mixture. Pulse for a few seconds.
3. Add remaining beaten egg white mixture. Pulse for 5-6 seconds. Do not over-mix. It should be just folded into it.
4. Transfer to a greased loaf pan.
5. Bake in a preheated oven at 375º F for about 20-25 minutes or until done. A toothpick, when inserted in the center, should come out clean.
6. If you want to make muffins, then pour the batter into greased muffin tins.

# Low Carb Bagels

Serves: 12

Nutritional values per serving:
Calories –360, Fat –28 g, Carbohydrates –8 g, Protein –21 g

Ingredients:

- 3 cups almond flour
- 5 cups mozzarella cheese, shredded
- 4 large eggs, beaten
- 2 tablespoons gluten free baking powder
- 4 ounces cream cheese, cubed
- Sesame seeds to top (optional)

Method:

1. Place parchment paper on a baking sheet and set aside.
2. Add almond flour and baking powder into a bowl. Stir and set aside.
3. Add mozzarella and cream cheese into a microwave safe bowl. Microwave on high for 2 minutes. Stir after a minute of cooking.
4. Remove from the microwave and stir again.
5. Add almond flour mixture and eggs into the bowl of cheese. Mix with your hands. Knead until dough is formed. If the dough is too hard to knead, then place in the microwave for about 20 seconds to heat.
6. Divide the dough into 12 equal parts. Roll each portion like a log. Then press the ends of the log together to form a bagel. Place it on the prepared baking sheet.
7. Repeat with the remaining 11 parts. Bake in batches if required.

8. Bake in a preheated oven at 400º F for about 10-15 minutes or until light brown on top and firm to touch.

# Meat Bagel

Serves: 12

Nutritional values per serving:
Calories –457, Fat –35.7 g, Carbohydrates –4.03 g, Protein –28.4 g

Ingredients:

- 4 pounds ground pork
- 3 medium onion, finely chopped
- 1 1/3 cup tomato sauce
- 4 large eggs
- 2 tablespoons butter or ghee
- 2 teaspoons paprika
- 1 teaspoon pepper powder
- 2 teaspoons salt
- Toppings of your choice

Method:
1. Place a skillet over medium heat. Add ghee or butter. When it melts, add onions and sauté until translucent. Turn off the heat and cool completely.
2. Add onions into a bowl and add rest of the ingredients and mix until well combined.
3. Divide into 12 equal portions and shape into bagels.
4. Place in a baking dish that is lined with parchment paper.
5. Bake in a preheated oven at 400º F for about for about 40 minutes or until done.
6. Slice the bagels. Fill with toppings of your choice and serve. Nutritional value of toppings is not included.

# Low Carb Pizza Crust

Makes – 2 crusts of 8 slices each

Nutritional values per slice:
Calories –211, Fat –19 g, Carbohydrates –6 g, Protein –8 g

Ingredients:

- 4 cups almond flour
- 4 large eggs
- 4 tablespoons coconut oil
- 1 teaspoon sea salt

Method:

1. Add all the ingredients into a bowl. Mix to form a dough. Divide into 2 equal portions.
2. Place one portion on to a sheet of parchment paper. Place another parchment paper on top of the dough and roll until ¼ inch thick.
3. Remove the parchment paper that is on the top. Place the crust in a pizza pan. Prick at several places with a fork.
4. Bake in a preheated oven at 400º F for about 15-20 minutes or until light brown.
5. Repeat steps 2-4 with the remaining dough.

# Low Carb Pizza

Serves: 12

Nutritional values per serving:
Calories –266.8, Fat –21.4 g, Carbohydrates –3.5 g, Protein –15.1 g

Ingredients:

For pizza crust:

- 6 ounces cream cheese, softened
- ½ cup heavy cream
- 2 teaspoons chives
- ½ teaspoon garlic powder or 1 teaspoon garlic paste
- 6 eggs
- 1/3 cup Parmesan cheese, grated
- 3 cups mozzarella cheese, shredded
- 1 teaspoon Italian seasoning or pizza seasoning

For topping:

- ¾ cup keto friendly low carb pizza sauce or as required
- Toppings of your choice (low carb)
- 1 ½ cups mozzarella cheese, shredded

Method:

1. To make crust: Add cream cheese and egg to a bowl and beat well with an electric mixer until smooth. Add heavy cream, Parmesan, chives, pizza seasoning, and garlic.
2. Grease a baking dish and place mozzarella cheese in it. Spread it all over the pan. Pour cream cheese mixture over it.

3. Bake in a preheated oven at 375º F for about 20-25 minutes or until done
4. Remove from the oven. Spread pizza sauce over it. Place toppings of your choice over it.
5. Sprinkle remaining cheese on top. Bake until the cheese melts.
6. Cut into wedges and serve.

# 2-Minute Low Carb English Muffins

Serves: 4

Nutritional values per serving: ½ large slice or 1 small muffin
Calories –222, Fat –19.4 g, Carbohydrates –4.8 g, Protein –8.3 g

Ingredients:

Wet ingredients:

- 4 tablespoons cashew butter or almond butter
- 2 eggs, beaten
- 2 tablespoons almond milk
- 2 tablespoons butter

Dry ingredients:

- 4 tablespoons almond flour
- 1 teaspoon baking powder
- ¼ teaspoon salt

Method:

1. Add all the dry ingredients into a bowl. Add eggs and milk and whisk well.
2. Spray 4 ramekins with cooking spray. Set aside.
3. Add almond butter and butter into a microwave safe dish. Microwave on high for 30 seconds or until melted. Mix well. Let it cool.
4. Add the almond butter mixture into the mixture and mix until well combined.
5. Pour into the ramekins.
6. Microwave on high for 2 minutes.
7. When done, let it cool in the ramekins for a few minutes.

8. Serve as it is or toast and serve.

# Flourless Egg And Cottage Cheese Savory Breakfast Muffins

Serves: 6

Nutritional values per serving:
Calories –143, Fat –10 g, Carbohydrates –6 g, Protein –9 g

Ingredients:

Dry ingredients:

- ¼ cup almond meal
- ¼ cup Parmesan cheese, finely grated
- 2 tablespoons nutritional yeast flakes
- ¼ teaspoon Spike seasoning or any other all-purpose seasoning (optional)
- ¼ cup raw hemp seeds
- 2 tablespoons flaxseed meal
- ¼ teaspoon baking powder
- 1/8 teaspoon salt or to taste

Wet ingredients:

- 3 eggs, beaten
- 1 green onion, thinly sliced
- ¼ cup low fat cottage cheese

Method:

1. Add all the dry ingredients into a bowl and mix until well combined.
2. Add all the wet ingredients into a large bowl and whisk well.
3. Add the dry ingredients into the bowl of wet ingredients, a little at a time and whisk each time.

4. Spoon the batter into greased muffin molds. Fill up to ¾.
5. Bake in a preheated oven at 375º F for about 25 minutes or a toothpick. when inserted in the center, comes out clean.
6. Remove from the oven and place on a cooling rack to cool. Run a knife around the edges of the muffins and carefully remove the muffins.
7. It can be refrigerated for up to a week.

# Morning Meatloaf

Serves: 8

Nutritional values per serving:
Calories –682, Fat –56 g, Carbohydrates –5 g, Protein –38 g

Ingredients:

- 12 large eggs, lightly beaten
- ½ yellow onion, chopped
- 2 cups cheddar cheese, shredded
- 2 pounds bulk sweet Italian sausage or breakfast sausage
- 8 ounces cream cheese, at room temperature, divided
- 4 tablespoons scallions
- Melted ghee to grease

Method:
1. Grease a loaf pan with ghee and set aside.
2. Add eggs, onion, sausage and half the cream cheese into a bowl and mix until well combined.
3. Transfer the meat mixture into the prepared loaf pan.
4. Bake in a preheated oven at 375º F for about 25-30 minutes or until firm.
5. Remove the loaf pan from the oven and let it rest for 5 minutes. Trim off any fat that may have settled on the top.
6. Top with remaining cream cheese. Spread it all over. Sprinkle cheddar cheese and scallions.
7. Place the loaf pan back into the oven. Bake for 5 minutes.
8. After that broil for 2-3 minutes or until the way, you like the cheese to be browned.
9. Remove from the oven and let it rest for 5-10 minutes.

10. Slice and serve.

# Low Carb Meat Loaf

Serves: 6

Nutritional values per serving:
Calories –409, Fat –33 g, Carbohydrates –5 g, Protein –23 g

Ingredients:

- ¼ cup almond flour
- 1 tablespoon butter
- ½ pound Italian sausage
- 1 pound ground beef
- 3 cloves garlic, minced
- 1 large egg
- ¼ cup dry Parmesan cheese, grated
- 4 ounces white onion, chopped
- ½ cup green pepper, chopped
- 2 tablespoons fresh parsley, chopped or 1 tablespoon dried parsley
- 1 tablespoon fresh thyme leaves, chopped or ½ tablespoon dried thyme
- 1 tablespoon fresh basil leaves, chopped or ½ tablespoon dried basil
- ½ teaspoon salt
- Pepper powder to taste
- 1 tablespoon low carb keto friendly barbecue sauce
- 1 teaspoon Dijon mustard
- ¼ teaspoon gelatin, unflavored
- 2 tablespoons heavy cream

Method:

1. Add almond flour and Parmesan into a bowl and whisk. Keep it aside.
2. Place a skillet over medium heat. Add butter. When butter melts, add onions, garlic and green pepper. Sauté until onions are translucent. Remove from heat and let it cool.
3. Add cooled mixture into the food processor and pulse until vegetables are minced.
4. Whisk together egg, salt, pepper, mustard, barbeque sauce, and cream. Sprinkle gelatin over the egg mixture and keep aside for 5 minutes.
5. Add minced vegetables and mix well.
6. Mix together ground beef and sausage in a large bowl until there are no large lumps. The meat should not be kneaded for more than 5 minutes. The meat will become tough otherwise.
7. Add egg mixture and mix. Now add the almond flour mixture.
8. Just in case your mixture is sticky, add some more Parmesan cheese. Add about a tablespoon at a time and mix until meat does not stick.
9. Grease a glass baking dish with a little butter. Place the meat mixture into the glass dish and shape into a loaf. Make sure to leave about an inch of space on all the sides of the glass dish.
10. Bake in a preheated oven at 350º F for about an hour until the loaf is brown and a cooking thermometer, when inserted in the center of the loaf, shows 160º F.
11. Remove from oven and cool for a while. Slice and serve.

# Keto Breadsticks

Serves: 10 (4 breadsticks per serving)

Nutritional values per serving:
Calories –334, Fat –26.9 g, Carbohydrates – 16 g, Protein –12.8 g

Ingredients:

For tortilla dough:

- 2 cups almond flour
- ½ cup coconut flour
- 4 tablespoons chia seeds, ground
- 1 ½ cups flaxseed meal
- 4 tablespoons whole psyllium husk or 2 tablespoons psyllium husk powder
- 2 cups lukewarm water + extra if required
- 2 teaspoons salt

For topping:

- 4 large yolks or melted ghee
- 2 teaspoons coarse sea salt or pink Himalayan salt
- 8 tablespoons mixed seeds of your choice like poppy seeds, caraway seeds or sesame

To serve (optional): Use any, as required

- Pesto of your choice
- Basil –macadamia pesto
- Red pesto
- Keto friendly BBQ sauce
- Keto friendly cheese sauce
- Keto friendly marinara sauce

Method:

1. To make breadsticks: Add all the ingredients of tortilla dough into a bowl and knead into dough.
2. Cover and refrigerate for about 20-25 minutes.
3. Line a baking sheet with parchment paper. Set aside.
4. Remove the dough from the refrigerator.
5. Make into around equal portions. Moisten your hands with water and roll the dough into long breadsticks of about 8-10 inches long.
6. Place the breadsticks on the prepared baking sheet. Brush with either yolks or melted ghee.
7. Sprinkle the seeds on it. Press it lightly the seeds on to the sticks.
8. Bake in a preheated oven at 350º F for about 15-20 minutes until crisp and brown or according to the way you like them.
9. Serves with the topping options of your choice. Nutritional values of toppings not included.

# Cheesy Cauliflower Breadsticks

Serves: 16

Nutritional values per serving:
Calories –185, Fat –13.32 g, Carbohydrates –3.36 g, Protein – 13.32 g

Ingredients:
- 8 cups cauliflower, grated to rice like texture
- 4 cups mozzarella cheese, shredded + 2 cups extra to top
- 3 teaspoons garlic, minced
- 2 teaspoons red pepper flakes or to taste
- Pepper to taste
- 6 teaspoons Italian seasoning or dried oregano
- Kosher salt to taste
- 2 eggs, beaten

Method:
1. Add cauliflower rice to a microwave safe bowl and cover with a lid. Microwave on high for 10 minutes. Transfer into a bowl. Alternately you can steam the cauliflower.
2. Grease a large baking sheet with cooking spray. Place parchment paper over it. Use 2 baking sheets if required.
3. After cooking, if you find that there is too much moisture in the cauliflower, place some paper towels over it to absorb some of the moisture.
4. Add garlic, red pepper flakes, salt and Italian seasoning. Mix well.
5. Add beaten eggs and mozzarella cheese. Mix well.

6. Transfer the mixture on to the prepared baking sheet. Press well. Bake in a preheated oven at 425°F for 30 minutes or until golden brown in color.
7. Remove from oven. Sprinkle 2 cups mozzarella cheese all over the crust.
8. Bake for another 8-10 minutes.
9. Remove from oven. Cut into sticks.
10. Serve hot.

# Oopsies

Serves: 16

Nutritional values per serving:
Calories −68, Fat −6 g, Carbohydrates −0.7 g, Protein −2.8 g

Ingredients:

- 6 eggs, separated
- 1 teaspoon baking powder
- 7 ounces cream cheese
- 1/8 teaspoon salt

Method:

1. Line a baking sheet with parchment paper and set aside.
2. Beat the whites until stiff peaks are formed. Set aside.
3. Beat the yolks. Add cream cheese and beat until smooth and well combined.
4. Add baking powder and mix well.
5. Add whites into the bowl of yolks and fold gently until well combined.
6. Drop large spoonfuls of mixture on the prepared baking sheet. Leave a gap between 2 Oopsies.
7. Bake in a preheated oven at 350°F for about 5-10 minutes or until done.

# Aip Bread Rolls

Serves: 8

Nutritional values per serving:
Calories −200, Fat −16 g, Carbohydrates −11 g, Protein −3 g

Ingredients:

- ½ cup coconut oil, melted
- 1 teaspoon baking soda
- 1 teaspoon salt
- 1 ½ cups hot water
- 1 ½ cups coconut flour
- 4 tablespoons Italian seasoning
- 8 tablespoons gelatin

Method:

1. Add coconut oil, coconut flour, and baking soda into a bowl and mix well. Add Italian seasoning and salt and stir.
2. Add hot water into a bowl. Add gelatin into it. Mix well. Set aside for 2-3 minutes.
3. Add the gelatin mixture into the coconut flour mixture and mix well to form a dough.
4. Divide the dough into 8 equal portions. Shape into balls. Then roll the ball between the palms of your hands into a log. Repeat with the remaining portions.
5. Place on a greased baking sheet that is lined with parchment paper.
6. Bake in a preheated oven at 300°F for about 45 minutes.
7. Remove from oven and cool for a while. Brush with melted ghee or butter and serve.

# Dinner Roll

Serves: 5

Nutritional values per serving:
Calories –102, Fat –7 g, Carbohydrates –5.8 g, Protein –3 g

Ingredients:

Dry ingredients:

- ¼ cup coconut flour
- ¼ teaspoon salt
- ¼ teaspoon baking powder
- ¼ cup psyllium husk powder

Wet ingredients:

- 6 tablespoons water
- 2 tablespoons butter
- 2 large eggs

Method:

1. Add all the dry ingredients into a bowl and mix well.
2. Add eggs into a mixing bowl. Beat well with an electric mixer. Add butter and water and beat until well combined.
3. Add the mixture of dry ingredients and beat until the mixture is thick and well combined.
4. Divide the dough into 5 equal portions. Shape into balls. Then roll the ball between the palms of your hands into a log. Repeat with the remaining portions.
5. Place on a greased baking sheet that is lined with parchment paper.
6. Bake in a preheated oven at 350°F for about 30-35 minutes.

# Keto Buns

Serves: 20 buns

Nutritional values per bun:
Calories –208, Fat –15.2 g, Carbohydrates –12.4 g, Protein –10.1 g

Ingredients:

Dry ingredients:

- 3 cups almond flour or almond meal
- 1 cup coconut flour
- 2/3 cup psyllium husk powder (powder the psyllium husk)
- 1 cup flax meal
- 1 ½ tablespoons onion powder
- 2 teaspoons baking soda
- 10 tablespoons sesame seeds
- ½ tablespoons cream of tartar
- 1 ½ tablespoons granulated garlic
- 2 teaspoons sea salt

Wet ingredients:

- 4 large eggs
- 12 large egg whites
- 4 cups boiling water

Method:

1. Mix together all the dry ingredients except the sesame seeds in a bowl.
2. Add the egg whites and eggs and whisk well until thick dough is formed.

3. Add boiling water and mix until well combined.
4. Spoon about 2 tablespoons of the batter for each bun on to a nonstick baking tray that is lined with parchment paper. Leave a gap between 2 buns.
5. Press the sesame seeds on to the buns.
6. Bake in a preheated oven at 350°F for about 30-35 minutes or until done.
7. Remove the tray from the oven. When it is slightly cooled, transfer on to a wire rack to cool completely.
8. Brush with butter or cream cheese or any other topping of your choice. Nutritional values of the topping not included.

# Strawberry Shortcake

Serves: 10

Nutritional values per serving:
Calories –273.2, Fat –25.96 g, Carbohydrates –4.42 g, Protein – 6.64 g

Ingredients:

For keto puff cakes:

- 6 large eggs, separated
- ½ teaspoon baking powder
- 4 tablespoons erythritol
- ½ teaspoon vanilla extract
- 6 ounces cream cheese

For filling:

- 2 cups heavy cream, whipped
- 20 strawberries, chopped

Method:

1. Beat egg whites with an electric mixer until soft peaks are formed.
2. Add yolks, vanilla, cream cheese, erythritol and baking powder into another bowl.
3. Beat again until well combined. Add egg whites to the cream cheese mixture. Fold gently.
4. Spread on a lined baking sheet.
5. Bake in a preheated oven at 300°F for about 30-35 minutes or until done.

6. Cool for at least an hour before serving.
7. Chop into 20 equal squares.
8. Mix together cream and strawberries.
9. Sandwich the strawberry cream mixture between 2 squares of shortcake and serve.

# Blueberry Lemon Muffins

Serves: 30

Nutritional values per serving:
Calories –184, Fat –17 g, Carbohydrates –6 g, Protein –5 g

Ingredients:

- 4 cups almond flour
- 4 eggs
- 10 packets artificial sweeteners such as Splenda or stevia or more to taste
- 2 teaspoons lemon extract or flavoring
- 1 teaspoon salt
- ¼ cup butter, melted
- ¼ teaspoon baking soda
- 1 teaspoon dried lemon zest
- 2 ounce fresh blueberries
- 2 cups heavy cream

Method:
1. Line 30 muffin molds with cupcake papers or liners.
2. Add flour and cream into a bowl. Whisk well. Add eggs, one at a time and whisk each time.
3. Add rest of the ingredients and mix well.
4. Fill the batter into the muffin molds up to ½.
5. Bake in a preheated oven at 350°F for about 20 minutes or until a toothpick when pierced in the center comes out clean.

6. Cool completely. Tastes best when served with butter.

# Chocolate Covered Macaroons

Serves: 24

Nutritional values per serving:
Calories –73, Fat –7.3 g, Carbohydrates – 2.7 g, Protein –1 g

Ingredients:

- 2 large egg whites
- 1 teaspoon almond extract
- 1 ½ ounces sugar-free chocolate
- 2 cups shredded coconut, unsweetened
- A large pinch salt
- ½ cup erythritol
- 4 tablespoons coconut oil

Method:

1. Place shredded coconut on a parchment paper lined baking sheet. Spread it all over the sheet.
2. Bake in a preheated oven at 350°F for about 4-5 minutes until toasted.
3. Whisk egg whites until frothy and doubled in volume. Add erythritol and salt and whisk again. Add almond extract and toasted coconut.
4. Divide the mixture into 8 equal portions. Shape each portion balls and place on the prepared baking sheet.
5. Bake in a preheated oven at 350°F for about 15 minutes until golden brown in color.
6. Meanwhile, melt coconut oil and chocolate in a double boiler. Whisk until well combined.
7. Remove from heat. Drizzle this over each of the macaroons.

8. Cool completely and serve.

# Pesto Keto Crackers

Serves: 12

Nutritional values per serving:
Calories –210, Fat –20 g, Carbohydrates –5.5 g, Protein –5 g

Ingredients:

Dry ingredients:

- 2 ½ cups almond flour
- 1 teaspoon salt
- ½ teaspoon dried basil
- ½ teaspoon ground black pepper
- 1 teaspoon baking powder
- ½ teaspoon cayenne pepper or to taste

Wet ingredients:

- 2 cloves garlic, peeled, pressed
- 6 tablespoons butter, chopped into small pieces
- 4 tablespoons basil pesto

Method:

1. Place parchment paper over a large baking sheet. Set aside. Use 2 baking sheets if required.
2. Mix together all the dry ingredients in a large bowl.
3. Add basil and mix until coarse crumbs are formed.
4. Add butter and mix with your hands until dough is formed.
5. Spread the dough on the prepared baking sheet evenly such that it is about 1 ½ mm in thickness. Use 2 baking sheets if required.

6. Bake in a preheated oven at 325°F for about 15 minutes until light golden brown.
7. Remove from the oven and chop into 12 equal crackers or into smaller crackers if desired.
8. Store in an airtight container at room temperature. It can last for a week.

# Cheesy Party Crackers

Serves: 4 (16 crackers)

Nutritional values per serving of 4 crackers:
Calories –168, Fat –13.4 g, Carbohydrates –6.3 g, Protein –8.4 g

Ingredients:

Dry ingredients:

- ½ cup almond flour
- 1 tablespoon whole psyllium husk
- ½ teaspoon sea salt or Himalayan pink salt
- Pepper to taste
- ¼ cup flax meal

Wet ingredients:

- ½ cup water
- ½ cup Parmesan cheese, grated

Method:

1. Place parchment paper over a large baking sheet. Set aside.
2. Mix together all the dry ingredients in a bowl. Add cheese and mix well.
3. Add water and mix with your hands until dough is formed. Let the dough rest for 12-15 minutes.
4. Spread the dough on the prepared baking sheet evenly such that it is about 1 ½ mm in thickness. Use 2 baking sheets if required.
5. Bake in a preheated oven at 325°F for about 15 minutes until light golden brown.
6. Remove from the oven and chop into 16 equal crackers or into smaller crackers if desired.

7. Store in an airtight container at room temperature. It can last for a week.

# Microwave Bread (1)

Serves: 8 slices

Nutritional values per serving: 1 slice

Calories –132, Fat –13 g, Carbohydrates –2 g, Protein –3.25 g

Ingredients:

- 2/3 cup almond flour
- ¼ teaspoon salt
- 1 teaspoon baking powder
- 5 tablespoons ghee or butter or coconut oil, melted
- 2 eggs, beaten

Method:

1. Add all the ingredients into a microwave safe bowl. Whisk well.
2. Microwave on High for 90 seconds.
3. Cool for a while.
4. Slice and serve.

# Cinnamon Swirl Bread

Serves: 24

Nutritional values per serving:
Calories –174, Fat –17 g, Carbohydrates –5 g, Protein –5 g

Ingredients:

For cinnamon mix:

- 2 teaspoons ground cinnamon
- 2 tablespoons Pyure all-purpose

Dry ingredients:

- 1 1/3 cup almond flour
- 1 teaspoon xanthan gum
- 2/3 cup coconut flour
- 2 teaspoons ground cinnamon
- 1 teaspoon salt
- 1 cup swerve or erythritol
- ½ teaspoon stevia extract powder
- 2 teaspoons baking powder

Wet ingredients:

- 1 cup butter, melted
- 14 large eggs
- 6 tablespoons coconut oil, melted
- 2 teaspoons vanilla extract

Method:

1. To make cinnamon mix: Add Pyure and cinnamon in a bowl. Stir and set aside.
2. For bread: Add all the dry ingredients into a bowl and mix well.
3. Add all the wet ingredients into the food processor. Pulse until well combined.
4. Add the dry ingredients and pulse until a smooth batter is formed.
5. Take out 1 cup of the batter and add into the cinnamon mix. Stir and set aside.
6. Take a loaf pan and line with parchment paper. Pour half the bread batter into it. Spread it uniformly.
7. Spread half the cinnamon mix batter over the bread batter and spread it uniformly.
8. Pour remaining bread batter over it. Finally, top with the remaining cinnamon mix batter. Take a knife and swirl the batter lightly.
9. Bake in a preheated oven at 350°F for about 40 minutes. Then lower the temperature to 325°F. If you find the top is getting brown and is not cooked inside, then cover the loaf pan with foil. Bake for 15 minutes or until a toothpick inserted in the center comes out clean.
10. Let it rest in the oven for 10-15 minutes.
11. Remove from the oven and cool for some more time. Slice and serve.

# Keto Bread Loaves Bread

Serves: 16

Nutritional values per serving:
Calories –154, Fat –8.5 g, Carbohydrates –11.3 g, Protein –9.23 g

Ingredients:

- 12 large eggs, at room temperature
- 1 cup flax meal
- 2 cups coconut flour
- 1 teaspoon baking soda
- 2 teaspoons baking powder
- 2 teaspoons salt
- 1 cup water
- 2 tablespoons apple cider vinegar

Method:

1. Add all the ingredients to the food processor bowl. Pulse until the mixture is well combined.
2. Transfer to a greased loaf pan.
3. Bake in a preheated oven at 350º F for about 40 minutes or until done.
4. Cool for a couple of hours. Slice and serve warm.

# Focaccia Style Flax Bread

Serves: 6

Nutritional values per serving:
Calories –134, Fat –8.8 g, Carbohydrates –6.5 g, Protein –5.9 g

Ingredients:

- 1 cup flax seeds, roughly ground
- ½ tablespoon Italian herb mix
- 3 medium eggs
- 2 ½ tablespoons avocado oil or light olive oil
- ¼ cup water
- ½ tablespoon baking powder
- ½ teaspoon sea salt

Method:

1. Line a baking pan with parchment paper on the bottom as well as the sides.
2. Add flax seeds, baking powder, Italian herb mix and salt into a bowl. Mix well and set aside.
3. Add eggs, oil, and water into a blender. Blend for 30-40 seconds until smooth. Pour into the bowl of flaxseed mixture.
4. Mix until well combined. Pour into the prepared baking pan. Spread with the back of the spatula evenly.
5. Bake in a preheated oven at 350º F for about 20 minutes or until the top is golden brown.
6. Chop into 6 pieces and serve.

# Coconut Tortillas

Serves: 18-20

Nutritional values per serving:
Calories –63, Fat –4 g, Carbohydrates –6 g, Protein –5 g

Ingredients:

- 1 cup coconut flour
- 2 ½ cups almond milk, unsweetened
- 10 large eggs
- 1 teaspoon sea salt
- Cooking spray

Method:

1. Add all the ingredients into a bowl. Whisk well. Set aside for 5 minutes. The batter should pour easily and runny. Add more milk or eggs in equal quantities if required.
2. Place a small skillet or pan over medium heat. Spray with cooking spray. Pour ¼ cup of the prepared batter into the skillet. Swirl the pan so that the batter spreads evenly.
3. Cover and cook until the edges begin to get golden brown. Flip sides. Cover and cook until done.
4. Repeat with the remaining batter to make remaining tortillas.

# Almond Flour Tortillas

Serves: 12

Nutritional values per serving:
Calories –, Fat – g, Carbohydrates – g, Protein – g

Ingredients:

- ½ cup psyllium husk, ground
- 1 teaspoon sea salt
- 4 tablespoons coconut flour
- 2 cups almond flour
- ½ teaspoon baking powder
- ½ cup hot water + extra if required
- 2 tablespoons avocado oil or olive

Method:

1. Add all the dry ingredients into a bowl and mix.
2. Add ½ cup hot water and mix to form a dough. Add more hot water if you find the dough too hard or dry.
3. Divide the mixture into 12 equal portions. Shape each into balls.
4. Roll the balls into flat shape like tortillas.
5. Heat pancake grill to 350º F and grill the tortilla until done.
6. Repeat with all the tortillas.

# Cheesy Garlic Bread

Serves: 10

Nutritional values per serving:
Calories –175, Fat –16 g, Carbohydrates –4 g, Protein –8 g

Ingredients:

Dry ingredients:

- 2 ½ cups almond flour
- 4 teaspoons baking powder
- ½ teaspoon salt
- 2 tablespoons coconut flour
- 1 teaspoon xanthan or guar gum (optional)
- ½ teaspoon garlic powder

Other Ingredients:

- 6 egg whites, beaten until fluffy
- ½ cup warm water
- 4 tablespoons olive oil or avocado oil
- 2 teaspoons live yeast granules
- 2 teaspoons coconut sugar (optional)
- 1 cup mozzarella cheese, shredded

For topping:

- 2 cups mozzarella cheese, shredded
- ½ teaspoon salt
- 4 tablespoons butter, melted
- 1 teaspoon Italian seasoning
- ½ teaspoon garlic powder

Method:

1. To bake bread dough: Add all the dry ingredients into a bowl. Mix well.
2. Add warm water and sugar. Stir until sugar is dissolved. Sprinkle yeast and set it aside for a few minutes.
3. To the bowl of dry ingredients, add olive oil and the yeast mixture. Mix well with a rubber spatula. Add eggs and mix until well combined.
4. Add mozzarella and combine well.
5. Transfer the batter on to a parchment paper lined or greased large baking dish.
6. Bake in a preheated oven at 400º F for about 15 minutes or until the sides of the bread are turning golden brown.
7. Remove from the oven and keep aside to cool.
8. Mix together in a bowl, salt, butter and garlic powder. Brush this mixture over the bread.
9. Sprinkle mozzarella cheese over the bread. Season with Italian seasoning.
10. Bake for a few minutes until the cheese is melted.
11. Remove from the oven and let it rest for 10-12 minutes.
12. Slice and serve.

# Zucchini Bread

Serves: 32 slices

Nutritional values per serving: For 1 slice
Calories -174, Fat – 15.7 g, Carbohydrates – 13.8 g, Protein – 5 g

Ingredients:

Dry ingredients:

- 5 cups almond flour
- 3 cups erythritol
- 3 teaspoons baking powder
- ½ teaspoon ground ginger
- 2 teaspoons ground cinnamon
- 1 teaspoon ground nutmeg
- 1 teaspoon salt
- 1 teaspoon xanthan gum (optional)

Other Ingredients:

- 1 cup olive oil
- 2 teaspoons vanilla extract
- 1 cup walnuts chopped
- 2 cups zucchini, grated
- 6 large eggs

Method:

1. Add eggs, oil, and vanilla into a large bowl and whisk well. Set aside.
2. Add all the dry ingredients into another bowl.
3. Add the dry ingredients into the bowl of egg mixture and mix until well combined.

4. Squeeze out excess moisture from the zucchini.
5. Add zucchini and most of the walnuts and fold gently. Leave some walnuts for the top. Sprinkle remaining walnuts on top. Press the walnuts lightly on to the
6. Pour into a large greased loaf pan or use 2 loaf pans and bake in batches if required.
7. Bake in a preheated oven at 350º F for about 60-70 minutes or until the top is brown.
8. Remove from the oven. Cool for a while.
9. Slice and serve.

# Low Carb Soft Pretzels

Serves: 6

Nutritional values per serving:
Calories –217, Fat –18 g, Carbohydrates –3 g, Protein –11 g

Ingredients:

- 1 ½ cups mozzarella cheese, shredded
- ¾ cup almond flour
- 1 egg, at room temperature
- 1 tablespoon warm water
- ½ tablespoon pretzel salt
- 2 tablespoons cream cheese
- 1 teaspoon xanthan gum
- 1 teaspoon dried yeast
- 1 tablespoon butter, melted

Method:

1. Add cream cheese and mozzarella cheese into a microwave safe dish. Microwave for a couple of minutes until melted. Stir every 30 seconds.
2. Add yeast and warm water into a bowl. Stir and let it rest for 2 minutes.
3. Add almond meal and xanthan gum in the stand mixer with dough hook attachment. Mix until well combined.
4. Add eggs, yeast mixture and ½ tablespoon melted butter and mix with the mixer.
5. Add the melted cheese mixture and mix until dough is formed.

6. Divide the dough into 6 equal portions. Roll each portion between your palms into a long log. Twist it and shape into a pretzel.
7. Place a cookie sheet that is lined with parchment. Leave sufficient gap between 2 pretzels.
8. Brush remaining butter over the pretzels. Sprinkle pretzel salt.
9. Bake in a preheated oven at 390º F for about 60-70 minutes or until the top is golden brown.
10. Remove from the oven. Cool for a while.

# Low Carb Bagel Dogs Or Pretzel Dogs

Serves: 4

Nutritional values per serving:
Calories –378, Fat –32 g, Carbohydrates –5 g, Protein –18 g

Ingredients:

- 4 hot dogs
- 1-ounce cream cheese
- ½ cup + 2 tablespoons almond flour
- ¾ cup mozzarella cheese, grated
- 1 medium egg
- 1 tablespoon whey protein isolate

For topping:

- 1 medium egg
- 1 teaspoon water
- Sesame seeds (optional)

Method:

1. Line a baking sheet with parchment paper. Place rack in the center of the oven.
2. Place hot dogs on paper towels. Pat them dry.
3. Add cream cheese and mozzarella cheese into a microwave safe dish. Microwave for a couple of minutes until melted. Stir every 30 seconds.
4. Add almond meal and whey protein in the stand mixer with dough hook attachment. Mix until well combined.
5. Add egg and mix with the mixer.
6. Add the melted cheese mixture and mix until dough is formed. The dough will be sticky in texture.

7. Remove the dough and place on plastic wrap. Wrap tightly and freeze for 10-15 minutes.
8. Divide the dough into 4 equal portions. Grease your hands with a little oil. Roll each portion between your palms into a long log. Wrap this around the hot dog. Start wrapping from about 2 cm from one end of the hot dog.
9. Place a cookie sheet that is lined with parchment. Leave sufficient gap between 2 pretzels.
10. For topping: Mix together in a bowl, egg, and water. Brush this over the pretzels. Press sesame seeds on it.
11. Bake in a preheated oven at 390º F for about 10-15 minutes or until the top is golden brown.
12. Remove from the oven. Cool for a while and serve.

# Mini Pancake Donuts

Serves: 44 mini donuts

Nutritional values per serving:
Calories –32, Fat –2.7 g, Carbohydrates –0.7 g, Protein –1.4 g

Ingredients:

- 6 ounces cream cheese
- ½ cup almond flour
- 2 teaspoons baking powder
- 2 tablespoons coconut flour
- 2 teaspoons vanilla extract
- 20 drops stevia
- 6 large eggs
- 8 tablespoons erythritol
- Coconut oil spray

Method:
1. Add all the ingredients into a mixing bowl. Beat with an electric mixer or immersion blender until smooth.
2. Preheat the mini donut maker. Spray with coconut oil spray. Spoon batter into the wells of the donut maker.
3. Cook for 3 minutes per side.
4. Remove donuts from the donut maker and cool for a while.
5. Repeat with the remaining batter to make donuts.

# Chocolate Donuts

Serves: 16

Nutritional values per serving:
Calories –143.38, Fat –9.2 g, Carbohydrates –5.15 g, Protein – 10.51 g

Ingredients:

- 1 cup almond meal
- ½ teaspoon salt
- 2 teaspoons vanilla extract
- 4 tablespoons cocoa powder
- 4 tablespoons butter, melted
- 4 tablespoons heavy cream or almond milk
- 6 large eggs, separated
- ½ teaspoon baking powder
- ½ teaspoon ground cinnamon
- 1 cup Splenda
- 4 scoops 100% casein powder

Method:

1. Add whites into a large bowl. Beat until stiff peaks are formed.
2. Add yolks, Splenda, butter, and vanilla into another bowl. Whisk well. Add into the bowl of whites and fold gently.
3. Add all the dry ingredients into a third bowl. Mix well.
4. Add the dry ingredients mixture into the bowl of eggs. Mix until well combined.
5. Pour batter into donut pans up to ¾ in each well.

6. Bake in a preheated oven at 350º F for about 15 minutes or until a toothpick when inserted in the center comes out clean.

# Chocolate Waffles

Serves: 10

Nutritional values per serving:
Calories –289, Fat –26.6 g, Carbohydrates –7 g, Protein –7.2 g

Ingredients:

- 10 eggs, separated
- 3 ½ tablespoons cocoa, unsweetened
- 2 teaspoon baking powder
- 6 tablespoons full-fat milk or cream
- 3.8 ounces butter, melted
- 8 tablespoons coconut flour
- 8 tablespoons granulated sweetener of your choice
- 4 teaspoons vanilla extract

Method:

1. Add whites into a large bowl. Beat until stiff peaks are formed.
2. Add yolks, coconut flour, baking powder, sweetener and baking powder into another bowl. Whisk well.
3. Add butter slowly and whisk simultaneously until smooth. Add vanilla and milk and whisk again.
4. Add into the bowl of whites and fold gently. Do not beat it; just fold lightly.
5. Add the dry ingredients mixture into the bowl of eggs. Mix until well combined.
6. Preheat a waffle maker. Pour the batter into the waffle maker and cook until it is golden brown in color.
7. Repeat with the remaining waffles.

# Bread Crumbs

Serves: 2 cups breadcrumbs

Nutritional values per serving: 1 cup
Calories –652.3, Fat –61.67 g, Carbohydrates –13.36 g, Protein – 15.28 g

Ingredients:

- 2/3 cup almond flour
- 1 teaspoon baking powder
- 2 eggs whisked
- 2 tablespoons coconut flour
- ¼ teaspoon salt
- 5 tablespoons ghee or butter, melted

Method:

1. Add all the ingredients into a bowl. Whisk well.
2. Divide and pour into 2 mugs.
3. Microwave on High for 90 seconds.
4. Cool for a while.
5. Remove from the mug and break into pieces. Spread the pieces on a baking sheet.
6. Bake in a preheated oven at 350º F for about 5-10 minutes or until crisp.

# Garlic Bread

Serves: 5

Nutritional values per serving:
Calories –89, Fat –8 g, Carbohydrates –2 g, Protein –2 g

Ingredients:

For bread:

- ½ cup + 2 tablespoons almond flour
- 1 teaspoon baking powder
- 1 teaspoon apple cider vinegar or white vinegar
- 1 teaspoon sea salt
- ½ cup + 2 tablespoons boiling water
- 2 ½ tablespoons psyllium husk powder
- 2 whites from medium size eggs

For garlic butter:

- 2 ounces butter, at room temperature
- 1 tablespoon fresh parsley, finely chopped
- 1 small clove garlic, minced
- ¼ teaspoon salt

Method:

1. Add all the dry ingredients into a bowl and mix well.
2. Add vinegar, boiling water and whites into the bowl of dry ingredients and mix with a hand mixer to form a dough. Do not mix too much.
3. Divide the dough into 5 equal portions. Moisten your hands and roll into hot dog buns.

4. Place on a lined baking sheet. Leave sufficient gap between the buns while placing on the baking sheet.
5. Place on the lower rack.
6. Bake in a preheated oven at 350º F for about 40-50 minutes or until done.
7. Meanwhile, mix together all the ingredients of garlic butter into a bowl. Place in the refrigerator until the buns are baked.
8. Remove the buns from the oven and cool. Halve the buns. Spread the garlic butter on the cut halves of the buns.
9. Bake in a preheated oven at 425º F for about 10-15 minutes or until golden brown.

# Flourless Chocolate Cake

Serves: 16

Nutritional values per serving:
Calories –240, Fat –21 g, Net Carbohydrates –2 g, Protein – 5.6g

Ingredients:

- 8 ounces unsweetened bakers chocolate
- 2 cups erythritol divided into 3 portions of 1 cup, ½ cup, and ½ cup
- 1 cup cocoa powder
- 1 teaspoon salt
- 1 cup butter
- 6 eggs, separated
- 2 teaspoons vanilla extract

Method:

1. Add chocolate and butter into a heatproof bowl. Place the bowl of chocolate in double boiler. When Add 1 cup erythritol and mix until well combined. Remove from heat and keep it aside.
2. Whisk the egg whites until frothy. Add ½ cup erythritol slowly. Whisk simultaneously. Whisk until stiff peaks are formed.
3. Whisk yolks along with ½ cup of erythritol in another bowl. As you whisk, the yolks will turn pale yellow in color. Add melted chocolate mixture and stir until well combined.
4. Add cocoa powder and stir. Add about one-third of the beaten egg whites and fold gently. Repeat until all the egg whites are folded in. Don't over mix; fold the mixture gently.
5. Pour the batter into a greased baking dish.

6. Bake in a preheated oven at 350º F for about 35 minutes or until a knife when inserted in the cake comes out clean. Cool for a while.
7. Sprinkle some erythritol powder on top.
8. Slice and serve.

# Low Carb Flat Bread

Serves: 5

Carbohydrates- 13 g

Ingredients:

Dry ingredients:

- 1 ½ cups + 2 tablespoons almond flour
- 2.5 tablespoons whey protein powder
- ¼ teaspoon garlic powder
- 1 teaspoon baking powder
- ¼ teaspoon salt

Wet ingredients:

- 2 large eggs
- 2 cups water
- 3 tablespoons coconut flour
- 2 cups olive oil or avocado oil

Method:

1. Add all the dry ingredients into a bowl.
2. Add all the wet ingredients into a large bowl. Whisk well.
3. Add the dry ingredients into the bowl of wet ingredients and mix well. A sticky dough will be formed.
4. Transfer on to a sheet of parchment paper. Place another sheet of parchment paper on it and roll the dough until the dough is about ½ inch in thickness.
5. Remove the top sheet of parchment paper and place the dough with the lower parchment paper on a baking sheet.
6. Bake in a preheated oven at 325º F for about 20-25 minutes or until firm.

7. Cool completely. Chop into 5 equal portions. Halve each portion. Place filling of your choice between 2 portions and serve.

# Coconut Flour Flatbread

Serves: 4

Ingredients:

- 3 tablespoons coconut flour
- 2 eggs
- ½ teaspoon baking powder
- 2 tablespoons coconut oil, melted
- ¼ teaspoon sea salt

Method:

1. Add all the dry ingredients into a bowl.
2. Add all the wet ingredients into a large bowl. Whisk well. Add the dry ingredients into the bowl of wet ingredients and mix well. Set aside for a while.
3. Place a parchment paper on a baking sheet. Spoon ¼ the batter on one side. Spread the batter into a round with a spatula. The size should be of a bun.
4. Leave a little gap and spread the remaining 3 flatbreads.
5. Bake in a preheated oven at 350º F for about 10 minutes

# Microwave Bread (2)

Makes – 4 ramekins

Ingredients:

- 1 ½ cups almond flour
- 4 tablespoons sunflower seeds or nuts of your choice, toasted, crushed lightly
- ½ teaspoon salt
- 3 teaspoons baking powder
- 3 tablespoons walnut oil, melted
- 8 tablespoons flaxseed meal
- 6 eggs, beaten

Method:

1. Add all the ingredients into a bowl. Whisk well.
2. Pour equally into greased ramekins.
3. Microwave on High for 80 seconds, one ramekin at a time.
4. Cool for a while.
5. Slice and serve.

# Breakfast Biscuit

Serves: 2

Ingredients:

- 2 tablespoons coconut flour
- A pinch sea salt
- 2 teaspoons ghee or unsalted butter, cold
- ¼ cup golden flaxseed meal
- 1 teaspoon baking powder
- 2 large eggs, beaten

Method:

1. Add all the dry ingredients into a bowl.
2. Add ghee and mix well until it gets a crumbly texture. Add egg and mix well.
3. Grease small ovenproof bowls or ramekins and add the mixture into the bowls.
4. Bake in a preheated oven at 350º F for about 20-25 minutes or until firm
5. Alternately, you can microwave it on high for about 55 seconds.

# Crackers

Serves: 6

Ingredients:

- 2 cups almond flour
- 1 teaspoon garlic powder
- Pepper to taste
- Salt to taste
- 4 eggs
- 4 tablespoons water
- 4 tablespoons butter, melted
- 2 tablespoons fresh rosemary, minced

Method:

1. Place parchment paper over a large baking sheet. Set aside. Use 2 baking sheets if required.
2. Mix together all the dry ingredients in a large bowl.
3. Add rosemary and mix until coarse crumbs are formed.
4. Add butter and mix with your hands.
5. Add water and butter and mix until dough is formed.
6. Spread the dough on the prepared baking sheet evenly such that it is about 1 ½ mm in thickness. Use 2 baking sheets if required.
7. Bake in a preheated oven at 325°F for about 6-8 minutes until light golden brown.
8. Remove from the oven and chop into equal squares.
9. Store in an airtight container at room temperature. It can last for a week.

# Herb Bread

Serves: 8

Ingredients:

- 3 cups blanched almond flour
- 4 tablespoons golden flaxseed meal
- 4 tablespoons coconut flour
- ¼ cup mixed fresh herbs of your choice, finely chopped
- 3 teaspoons baking soda
- ½ cup coconut oil, melted
- 10 eggs
- 2 tablespoons apple cider vinegar
- ½ teaspoons salt

Method:

1. Add all the dry ingredients into the food processor bowl. Pulse for a few seconds until well combined.
2. Add all the remaining ingredients and pulse until a smooth batter is formed.
3. Pour into a greased loaf pan.
4. Bake in a preheated oven at 350°F for about 6-8 minutes until light golden brown. A toothpick, when inserted in the center, should come out clean.
5. Slice and serve with some butter brushed on it.

# Fluffy Keto Pancake / Waffle

Serves: 8

Ingredients:

For batter:

- 8 ounces cream cheese, softened
- 4 teaspoons vanilla extract or sugar-free vanilla syrup
- 8 tablespoons coconut flour
- ½ teaspoon ground cinnamon (optional)
- Milk or half and half, as required
- 8 eggs
- 2 tablespoons swerve or erythritol
- 3 teaspoons baking powder

For pancakes only:

- 1 teaspoon extra baking powder

For waffles only:

- 2 tablespoons butter, melted (optional)

Method:

1. Add cream cheese, vanilla, eggs, swerve and cinnamon into the blender. Pulse for a few seconds until well combined.
2. Add rest of the ingredients and blend until smooth. Transfer into a bowl and set aside for a few minutes. Add more milk if the batter becomes too thick.
3. To make pancakes: Add the extra baking powder and mix well.
4. Place a griddle over medium heat. Spray with cooking spray. Pour about ¼ cup batter over it. Swirl the pan a bit so that the batter spreads slightly.

5. Cook until the underside is golden brown. Flip sides and cook the other side too.
6. Repeat with the remaining batter.
7. To make waffles: Pour batter into a preheated waffle iron. Cook until golden brown.
8. Brush some butter over it. Drizzle sugar-free syrup over it and serve.

# Carrot Cake Loaf

Serves: 12

Ingredients:

Dry ingredients:

- 4 cups almond flour
- ¼ teaspoon Himalayan pink salt
- 2 teaspoons baking powder
- 2 teaspoons baking soda
- 6 teaspoons coconut flour
- 1 teaspoon ground cinnamon

Wet ingredients:

- 4 tablespoons coconut oil, melted
- 4 tablespoons coconut oil
- 10 drops stevia or to taste
- 2/3 cup carrots, grated
- 2/3 cup apple sauce, unsweetened
- 2 teaspoons vanilla extract

Options: Use any

- 2/3 cup mini dark chocolate chips
- 2/3 cup walnuts, chopped

Method:

1. Add all the dry ingredients into a bowl. Mix well.

2. Add all the wet ingredients into a bowl. Mix well. Add the wet ingredients into the bowl of dry ingredients and mix well.
3. Add the optional ingredient that you are using.
4. Pour into a greased loaf pan.
5. Bake in a preheated oven at 350°F for about 20-25 minutes until light golden brown. A toothpick, when inserted in the center, should come out clean.
6. Slice and serve with some butter brushed on it.

# Rosemary Coconut Savory Bread

Serves: 12

Ingredients:

- 8 eggs
- ½ cup coconut milk
- ½ cup olive oil
- 2 teaspoons freshly ground rosemary
- 2 teaspoons coarse sea salt
- 1 ½ cups coconut flour
- 2/3 cup flax meal
- 2 teaspoons baking soda

Method:

1. Add eggs, coconut milk, rosemary and oil into a bowl. Whisk well with a hand mixer.
2. Add flax meal, soda and sea salt. Whisk until well combined.
3. Add coconut flour and stir until well combined.
4. Transfer the dough into a greased loaf pan.
5. Bake in a preheated oven at 350°F for about 45 minutes until light golden brown. A toothpick, when inserted in the center, should come out clean.

# Thanksgiving Bread

Serves: 8

Ingredients:

- 2 tablespoon ghee or fat of your choice
- 4 stalks celery, chopped
- 2 onions, chopped
- 1 cup coconut flour
- 3 cups almond flour
- 1 cup walnuts, chopped
- 2 teaspoons baking soda
- 20 fresh sage leaves, finely chopped
- ¼ teaspoon nutmeg, freshly grated
- 1 cup chicken broth
- 8 eggs
- 5-6 strips bacon, cooked, crumbled
- ½ teaspoon fine sea salt
- 2 tablespoons fresh rosemary, finely chopped

Method:

1. Place a pan over medium heat. Add ghee. When the ghee melts, add onion and celery and sauté until onions are translucent.
2. Add walnuts and sauté until toasted. Turn off the heat and set aside.
3. Add coconut flour, almond flour, baking soda, salt, sage, nutmeg, and rosemary into a bowl. Mix well.
4. Add the onion mixture, eggs, and chicken broth into the bowl and mix until well combined.
5. Add bacon and fold gently.

6. Pour into a greased loaf pan.
7. Bake in a preheated oven at 350°F for about 35 minutes until light golden brown. A toothpick, when inserted in the center, should come out clean.
8. Slice and serve with some butter brushed on it.

# Bulletproof Bread

Serves: 6

Ingredients:

- 12 pastured eggs, separated
- Butter to grease
- 1 cup grass fed bulletproof collagen protein

Method:

1. Place middle rack in the oven.
2. Grease 2 loaf pans with butter and set aside. Preferably use a ceramic pan.
3. Beat the whites with a hand mixer until stiff peaks are formed.
4. Add bulletproof collagen protein and yolks and beat on low until well combined.
5. Divide and pour the batter into the prepared loaf pans.
6. Bake in a preheated oven at 350°F for about 35 -40 minutes until light golden brown. A toothpick, when inserted in the center, should come out clean. Bake in batches if required.
7. Remove from the oven after a few minutes. Cool completely. The bread will fall back to normal height. Cut into slices.
8. To serve: Place a skillet over medium heat. Grease with butter. Toast the bread lightly and serve.

# Conclusion

Thank you again for purchasing this book!

I hope you found the recipes in this book helpful in your quest to find the right kind of bread that are keto compliant. All of these recipes are extremely simple and offer a wide range of varieties in bread that are low carb. You don't have to worry about gaining weight with these recipes, and can now eat bread guilt free.

www.ingramcontent.com/pod-product-compliance
Lightning Source LLC
Chambersburg PA
CBHW071442070526
44578CB00001B/191